the **Hidden Pain**

when you fear God is no longer
blessing your life

Amanda Manney

Copyright © 2019 Amanda Manney

All rights reserved. No part of this book may be reproduced, stored in a retrieval system, or transmitted in any form or by any means—electronic, mechanical, photocopy, recording, or otherwise—without written permission from the publisher except for brief quotations in printed reviews.

Edited by Rebekah Bogardus
Cover Photo: teamtime/DepositPhotos.com
Cover Design: Matt Manney
Layout: Matt Manney
Author Photo: Josh Berg Photography
Family Photo: Josh Berg Photography

Unless otherwise noted, all Scripture quotations are taken from the King James Version (KJV) in the Public Domain. Special emphasis in verses is added.

Scripture quotations marked MSG are taken from THE MESSAGE, copyright © 1993, 2002, 2018 by Eugene H. Peterson. Used by permission of NavPress. All rights reserved. Represented by Tyndale House Publishers, a Division of Tyndale House Ministries.

Disclaimer: The author and publisher have left out names and identifying details to protect the privacy of individuals. The author has tried to recreate events, locales and conversations from the author's memory of them. In order to maintain privacy the author and publisher have in some instances left out the name and identifying details of individuals. Although the author and publisher have made every effort to make sure all information is correct at press time, the author and publisher do not assume and hereby disclaim any liability to any party for any loss, damage, disruptions caused by stories with this book, whether such information is a result of errors or emission, accident, slander or other cause.

The author has put forth every effort to give proper credit to quotations and thoughts that are not original with the author. It is not their intent to claim originality with a quotation or thought that could not readily be tied to an original source.

— Dedication —

For my mom, whose life is an example of dealing with the hidden pain and still choosing to love and serve God.

Contents

1. The Fountain Dries Up — 7
2. A Wrong Life Principle — 11
3. Where Our Story Starts — 21
4. Depression and Failure — 31
5. The Night of Our Car Fire — 37
6. A Change of Heart — 49
7. Change and Criticism — 59
8. I Don't Owe an Explanation — 65
9. Starting Faithfully Stepping — 75
10. God is Still Molding Us — 85
11. The Bottom Drops Out — 93
12. Wrestling with God — 103

13. In the Midst of the Hidden Pain	117
14. Learning Longsuffering	123
15. Seeing God as My Father	133
16. Seven Don'ts God has Taught Me	143
17. Understanding the True Meaning of Success	157
18. Getting Back Up Again	167
19. Navigating the Storms	177
20. When God Doesn't Provide	183
21. My Story is Still Being Written	191
22. Rediscovering My Faith	199
23. Conclusion- It's Time to Soar	211
Bonus Chapter- How to Encourage Someone Going Through a Difficult Season	219
Acknowledgments	223
Endnotes	225
About the Author	229

Chapter One

The Fountain Dries Up

It was a beautiful summer day, the summer of 2011. I was outside walking (or should I say *waddling*) up and down driveways, passing out invitations to the church that my husband Matt and I would be starting in just a few weeks. I paused for a moment to catch my breath before climbing a rather steep driveway. As I paused, a little hand grabbed my hand and pulled, "Come on, Mommy. We have to put this on the door."

I looked down at my enthusiastic little blond-haired boy and smiled. He loved being outside, but he loved putting invitations on doors even more. This was his favorite thing to do. So as he pulled, I reluctantly began to climb the steep driveway.

Putting a hand on my swollen stomach, I felt our little girl kicking and squirming. We would get to meet her in just a few weeks. I couldn't wait. A little girl! We would have a boy and a girl! I smiled to myself as I walked up and placed the invitation on the door.

Our life was simply beautiful. Just a few months earlier, we had stepped out in faith, left everything familiar, and moved to a new town to start a church. God opened the windows of heaven and blessed us tremendously. He blessed us with money, gifts, resources, a down payment for our home, and more as we started this new chapter in our lives.

We bought our very first home. It wasn't huge, but it was ours! It was a cute brick home on a one-way street. It needed fixing up, and we had done just that. We worked really hard to make it our home. In just a few weeks, we would be bringing our little girl home to our new home and starting our church. I smiled again. Everything was working out perfectly. All our dreams were coming true.

Malachi and I turned around and began the steep descent down the driveway. As we did, my husband

The Fountain Dries Up

Matt called out to us, "Say cheese."

We looked up and smiled. *Snap*. Matt took a picture that is now forever cemented in my head. I still have that picture and look at it often. I looked so happy. It was a look of pure joy and idealism. Only God could have known how quickly the feelings I had on that bright summer day were going to change.

Within just a few short weeks, everything came crashing down. It was as if the fountain of God's blessing and favor had abruptly turned off and we didn't know how to turn it back on. We didn't know it at the time, but this was the feeling we would face and feel for the next eight years.

Chapter Two

A Wrong Life Principle

I have lived my entire life based on the overarching principle that if I obey God and follow Him, He will work everything out for me. Ever since high school, my life verse has been Psalm 18:30, "As for God, His way is perfect: the word of the Lord is tried: he is a buckler to all those that trust in Him." That verse has been a source of encouragement to me for the entirety of my life.

Another favorite verse of mine is Romans 8:28, "And we know that all things work together for good, to them who love God, to the who are the called according to his purpose." God can use the good and the bad in our lives to change us into who He wants us to be.

I always had what I would call a fairly "easy" life. Sure, I had hard things in my life – things I didn't understand and trials to walk through, but the overarching rule in my life was that if I did my part, God would do His part. With God's help, I breezed through elementary school, junior high, and senior high. I excelled in most areas of my life. I believed if I worked hard and honored God, He would "bless me." My idea of Him blessing me was success. I had that success. I was living a life true to God, and I was reaping the benefits of it.

After graduating high school, I left for college. College had its bumps and bruises, but for the most part, I did okay there too. I met and fell in love with my husband. We got married right after graduation and settled into serving on staff at a local church.

Once again, God blessed. We loved the church we served in. We both worked on staff and started a children's ministry as well as an addictions ministry while we were there. Both ministries were fairly successful, averaging attendance numbers over 100 for both. We spent five years serving on staff at this church and had our first child there.

Church Planting

In 2011, we headed into church planting with guns blazing. We loved God, and we were following His call on our lives. Certainly, *that* would give us His blessing! He would bless our ministry. It would grow quickly, and we would start satellite campuses, host large events and Bible studies, and show our community what God's love was all about.

So when everything fell apart before we even started, we couldn't have been more surprised, especially this Christian-school girl. I figured that like everything else in my life, it would all work out. If we just worked hard, prayed, and gave it enough time, everything would fall neatly into place. Boy, was I wrong!

It's taken the last eight years of getting our teeth kicked in to understand that my view of God and how He works and blesses in our lives was not exactly on point. A Bible conference I went to recently confirmed that thought.

An Old Testament Concept

The speaker for the day at this conference reminded us in great detail that the concept of following God and receiving His blessing is an Old Testament promise to the Jews. Over and over, God set a blessing and a curse before His people. They would receive His blessing if they obeyed Him. It was a one for one transaction. If they did right by God, He would bless them. If they didn't wholly follow God, He would punish them.

Then Jesus came on the scene in the New Testament and taught a very different concept. No longer does following God directly result in His divine blessing and protection. Jesus taught principals such as, "You reap what you sow," "the rain falls on the just and the unjust," and "in this world, you will have tribulation." The rules changed.

Think of the disciples. They gave up their professions to follow Jesus full time. Of all people, they should have received God's greatest blessings, yet they all died gruesome deaths. Peter was crucified upside down, Andrew was crucified, James was beheaded, Thomas was stabbed to death ... do you get the picture? John was the only disciple to die a natural death, and he died exiled to the Island of Patmos. The New Testament is full of other examples of men and women who followed Jesus but endured trials and struggles. Stephen was martyred for his faith, Paul was beaten several times and eventually beheaded, John the Baptist was beheaded, and many men and women were tortured and killed at the hands of the Romans.

In our heads, we understand the difference between how God dealt with the Jews in the Old Testament and how He deals with us as Christians today. In our hearts, however, we still subconsciously hold on to the Old Testament way of thinking.

What does this look like practically? Let me tell you what it looked like in my own life for the past eight years. (And if I am honest, sometimes it still trips me up.) For the past eight years, I have given everything I have to our church plant. I have loved on people, made meals for hurting and sick people, been at every service and activity, invited people into my home every week ... the list could go on and on. Surely God can see what I am doing for Him, right? Surely, He can see all I have sacrificed, right? Here's where it all falls apart though.

We have been on food stamps off and on. We have had months on end of not getting paid. Our salary places us in the "poverty" classification. We have had our hearts literally broken many times over by people who have hurt us and said horrible things to us and by friends who have walked away. We have weeks where there are five people sitting in the service and listening to Matt preach. We have spent money and hours of time preparing for events that nobody comes to.

That's confusing because it doesn't match the picture of how we see God working. I can't tell you how many times I have argued and pleaded with God to bless us, yet all I have felt is crushing defeat. There have been times I almost walked away from it all. The pressure, the hurt, the pain, the sense of failure, the needs, and the discouragement were all too much.

I am coming to the realization (I say *coming* because I am still working on this) that there are two fundamental flaws with this way of thinking. The first flaw is that this way of thinking is an Old Testament way of thinking. The second problem lies in the fact that I don't really understand what God's blessing truly is.

A Wrong Life Principle

My Personal Journey

I have been on an eight-year journey that has taken me in a completely different direction than I could have ever imagined. I'm not the same stars-in-my-eyes girl that I used to be. These last several years have come very close to destroying me and my faith. But that hasn't happened. I'm not the person I used to be, but I think that's a good thing. I've changed, and I'm going to continue to change. God is continuing to chisel away at all of the wrong parts of me. It's been painful ... scratch that ... it's been heart-wrenching. However, as I look back at the last eight years of my life, I know without a shadow of a doubt that some of the greatest blessings of my life have happened during these years.

I'm looking at two of them right now. My little girls, Maggie (age 5) and Macey (age 4), are playing house around me while I type in their room. Sometimes God sends His greatest blessings in the midst of our darkest days, and that is definitely true about these two crazy-but-precious girls who arrived during our church planting challenges. Malachi (age 9) and Madison (age 8) began our church-planting journey

the Hidden Pain

with us.

I certainly don't have all the answers. I'm in the midst of my own mess right now, but I have learned one thing over the past eight years – there is a type of pain that trumps most other types of pain in life. It's a kind of pain you can't really talk about. You can't share it with friends and family because it's too hard, and honestly, they don't usually understand it. This pain is the fear that maybe God is no longer blessing your life. Maybe your life isn't living up to God's standard, and He is withholding His blessing from your life. I call this *The Hidden Pain* because it's a pain so deep and private that it's totally hidden from the rest of the world.

I've dealt with this hidden pain for years. I've done everything in my power to serve God, be faithful, please Him, and love others with seemingly nothing in return. I felt that no matter what I did, God was obviously not pleased with me, and I must be doing something wrong for Him not to bless us. At times, I truly felt like God was against us. I felt like He was deliberately making things difficult for us.

I don't know if you have ever been there – the place

where you feel like God is no longer blessing your life. Since you picked up this book though, I'm assuming you have. It's a dark, lonely place to be. I want to give you hope because I so desperately needed hope when I was going through it myself. I begged God for help and encouragement. I read book after book, and I read my Bible for hours, journaled, prayed, and begged God for help but didn't find the answers I was looking for. I desperately needed to hear the words of this book. I wrote this book because I want to provide you with the encouragement and answers I didn't have when I needed them.

I believe there is hope for getting through a time like this in your life. I want to share with you what worked for me, what failed, and what I am still learning. To do that, I want to briefly run through my story so you can know how I got to the place of *The Hidden Pain* – the fear that God was no longer blessing my life. Let me take you back to the time before we started the church and what went wrong from there.

Chapter Three

Where Our Story Starts

Matt and I got married in 2006, and we settled into married life in Pennsylvania at the church where Matt had been working since graduating college. He graduated a year before me and started serving on staff at a large church. We worked together at that church for five years, running ministries for singles, children, and addicts. During that time, our first child, Malachi, was born.

Through those five years, we kept our singular focus in sight. We wanted to plant a church. Those five years were a test of faithfulness and patience while waiting for God to make it abundantly clear when we were to leave and start a church.

In January of 2011, our time finally came. Our pastor said that it was time for us to begin the process of starting a church. He asked that we pick a town somewhere between the church and Philadelphia, which was about an hour away. The Lord began to open doors quickly, and we got to work.

We spent about six months traveling to different churches, presenting our ministry, and getting financial support to start our church. During that time, God opened the windows of heaven and blessed us tremendously. Thousands of dollars flowed in for music books, printed materials, sound equipment, money for us to live on until the church could support us, and more. We were so excited to see what God was doing. We had an amazing building to meet in. Everything was going incredibly well. I was pregnant with our second child, and life couldn't get any better. Then everything came crashing down.

The Phone Call that Changed Everything

It started on a Tuesday – the Tuesday before our very first service. Matt received a call. A single call that changed everything.

The call came from the zoning officer of our town who told Matt in no uncertain terms—with a lot of yelling and cussing, actually—that we would not be allowed to use the building we were planning on for our church. We had cleared everything required for the zoning of our church building, but a slight discrepancy on the original blueprints of the building messed everything up.

In short, we had passed out more than ten thousand invitations and advertised a grand opening for a location we were no longer allowed to meet in. Stunned, Matt hung up the phone, and I will never forget the look on his face. What were we going to do? We had to come up with a new location in just five days!

Two days later after that phone call, I went into labor and had a rough delivery with our little girl, Madison. I missed the first service on Sunday. It was really just an open house because we hadn't secured a place to rent for services.

I didn't recover from childbirth as quickly as I would have liked. Not only that, but I seemed to be declining. I was in more pain each day instead of less. Not sure what was going on, I finally made an appointment with my doctor. The doctor confirmed what I was afraid of, I had a case of shingles. I was exhausted from all the work of getting ready for the start of our church and stressed from losing our location for services. The icing on the cake was my hard delivery with Madison. My body couldn't handle it all, and I went down.

Shingles hit me hard. It was much more painful than I had thought possible! It couldn't have come at a worse time with a newborn to take care of and nurse, an eighteen-month-old little boy who was very active, and a brand-new church plant. I couldn't sleep at night because of the pain, and I really struggled with the depression that came as a result of post-partum recovery combined with shingles.

Matt wasn't around much during this time as he was busy trying to fix the major problem we had – no building for our new church to meet in. When he was around, he was quiet and busy helping take care of our two little children. He knew I was in pain but didn't know what to do to fix it, and he hated that. He was frustrated and discouraged over the crushing blow of losing our building.

Securing a Building

Over the course of the next few weeks, Matt was able to secure a place for our church to rent. It wasn't ideal, but it would hold us over until we found something that better suited our needs. I slowly started to heal. Neither of us really knew what to say or think as we focused on just trying to stay afloat.

During that time, we became isolated, lonely, and discouraged. I remember thinking, "What did we do wrong? God, why are you punishing us?" This mindset is a very dangerous one, but I didn't see it at the time. I was hurt and confused, and Satan was beginning to sow seeds of doubting God's goodness in my mind.

Our New Normal

The next several months we just survived. I finally recovered, and we adjusted to our new normal. Our new normal consisted of setting up the church each and every week. Because we rented from another church, we had to work around their service schedule

the Hidden Pain

and building setup. We showed up at church every Sunday morning at 7:30, set up the nursery and kids' area, set up all of our sound and service equipment, and prepared for our service. Our service started at 8:30 a.m. and ended at 9:15. We had to put everything away and be off the premises by 9:30 when the other church started their services. We would get home from church by 9:45. It was crazy!

We weren't allowed to display any signs for our church on their property during the week. We could only place a small sign out front during the time we met on Sunday mornings. We began to see how difficult it was going to be to grow the church. Can I say *impossible*? It was practically impossible to grow the church! Sure, we passed out invitations every week and invited everyone we met to our church, but we saw very little growth. We tried to encourage ourselves that this was just for a short time—not more than a few months.

As it worked out though, we stayed in that church building much longer than we ever anticipated. We were there for four long years. During that time, babies number three and four were born. Maggie was born in

2014, and Macey came in 2015. We were so grateful and thankful for our growing family. We know children are a gift from God, and we thanked Him every day for ours. That was really the only sign of favor we received from the Lord during those years. Sundays ran together, the months ran together, and our hope that things would ever change began to fade.

The Danger of the In-Between

It's so easy to see God's Presence in the high moments of life such as when we get married, start a new job, receive a raise, have an incredible performance, bring home a baby, graduate with a new degree, etc. But during the lowest moments of life, it's much harder to see God. We question Him, call out to Him, ask for help, cry for relief, and spend more time seeking Him. We may not be able to clearly see Him, but we spend a considerable amount of time seeking Him and trying to get His attention.

However, I think the times in between the highs and the lows can be the most dangerous of all. It's the times in the middle when we are just living life – that's the danger zone. Nothing particularly bad is happening, but nothing particularly exciting is happening either. Days turn into weeks, weeks turn into months, and months turn into years, and all of a sudden, we don't realize how much time has gone by since we felt God's presence in our lives. I call this the danger zone because most people don't turn away from God on the mountaintops, those amazing moments in life. They realize the blessing they are receiving is from God.

Sometimes people turn away from God in the devastating moments in life. Something happens that rocks their faith, and they have a choice to either turn to God or turn away from Him. Most people recognize this though. They know the trying times of life have the capacity to make or break our relationship with God. Most of us are aware of it. Now we may still turn away from God when the pressure comes, but we aren't surprised by it.

The real danger lies during the in-between – the years when life happens and passes by without any deep connection between us and God. At least during the amazing moments and the horrible moments, we are aware of God and either turn to Him or turn away from Him. It's in the monotony of life where our faith is forged or broken.

How many people do you know who used to go to church and had a close relationship with the Lord but no longer do? You can't really pinpoint what happened or when they walked away; they just sort of drifted. Somewhere along the way, they stopped going to church, attending their small group, and reading their Bible. They simply just continued on with their life without even realizing it. I know far more people in this category than I do those who walked away from God because of a tragedy.

It's when life is just happening that we are in danger of walking away from God and our faith. When Matt and I were seeing God work in amazing ways and when we knew He was working in the difficulties we were walking through, we knew He was with us. When we went several years without feeling Him and without anything amazing or terrible happening, that was when we struggled the most. The monotony of life has the power to destroy our faith in God. The day-to-day living without supposedly "needing God" is far more dangerous to our relationship with Him.

It is during these times of vulnerability that we

must seek to actively engage with God. Spend time in prayer and Bible reading, get connected to a small group, and pull close to family and friends. When we simply exist, we are vulnerable and open to Satan's attacks because we don't see them coming.

Chapter Four

Depression and Failure

I remember one Sunday morning vividly. I had just finished playing the piano for the music service and the offertory. If I didn't have nursery or kids' class duty, I would usually get up from the piano and move to the front pew to sit and listen to Matt preach. Not that day. When I got done playing, I moved to one of the pews in the back of the auditorium. I looked around the room at the small handful of people sitting there and began to cry.

As Matt started to preach and I sat there, the tears began to flow. I didn't have the strength to hold them back. I was so weary. It wasn't a sleepy feeling; it was a "I'm so weary and discouraged and can't do this anymore" kind of feeling. I was at the end of myself. I told God I couldn't do it anymore. I was so tired of going nowhere. I was tired of hoping and praying every week that *next* week would be different. I was tired of hashing things out to determine what we could change or what we could do better only to never see anything change. That day I sat there empty and depleted. I was at the end of myself.

Have you ever been there? It's an achingly painful place to be. It's a place of such deep sadness and loneliness. I didn't feel like I could talk to anybody. I was a pastor's wife. I was supposed to have all the answers. I was supposed to be strong, but I had never felt like more of a failure in all my life. I felt like I didn't know who I was any more. I had no identity.

In her book *Uninvited,* Lysa TerKeurst said, "When my identity is tied to circumstances, I become extremely insecure because circumstances are unpredictable and ever changing. I rise and fall with successes and failures."[1] This was the perfect description of me. My identity was tied to the success or failure of our church. Our church was failing, so I must be a

Depression and Failure

failure as well.

I whispered to God that I couldn't do it anymore. I couldn't face anybody anymore. Matt and I were lonely, discouraged, and felt like failures. Had we made a mistake?

Were we not supposed to plant the church? We second-guessed ourselves daily. We tried to figure out what we were doing wrong. What were we supposed to learn?

We were doing and trying everything we knew and had been taught to grow a church. We held Sunday morning services, Sunday evening services, and a Wednesday night Bible study along with a kids' program. We ran Tuesday night visitation (a time when we would visit the homes of people who had attended our church). We went out every Saturday and invited people to our church. We mailed out invitations to our services. We had Easter Egg hunts, Harvest Festivals, Missions Conferences, Christmas programs, Vacation Bible Schools, special Sundays, kids' events, ladies' book studies, men's prayer breakfasts, and more. If you can think of it, we did it. We did all of those things with very little growth. We were so busy! We were working so hard but saw very little growth.

Just Try Harder

Before starting our church, every ministry we had ever been involved with had been successful, so we figured we just needed to try harder. How many times we believed this lie! We just kept telling ourselves to be more disciplined, host more events, talk to more people, work harder, etc. Yet this time, we were helpless. All the trying and striving was getting us nowhere. We couldn't fix this.

I remember sitting across from Matt many times on a date night or after dinner as we talked about what wasn't working and what needed to change to enable us to grow the church. We would pray and beg God to move the church forward, but no matter what, it just wouldn't grow.

Things Began to Get Worse

In spite of all our hard work and prayer, things didn't get better. In fact, they got worse. Over the next two years, the church continued to stagnate. People started getting frustrated with each other and with us.

Depression and Failure

Friends couldn't hang in there with us. Church members were weary and left in search of greener pastures in different churches. A few church members got angry with us for reasons that had nothing to do with us, but because we were already in a low place, we took the blame. We weren't mature enough to recognize that some people take out their frustration with life on their pastor.

During those early years, we were yelled at, received letters about how horrible a pastor and pastor's wife we were, and dealt with constant frustration from people.

I can't begin to tell you what this does to you as a person. Oh, the questions! *What are we doing wrong? Why are we so bad at this? Should we quit? Should we let someone else take over? Why is God not for us? Have we not prayed enough? Do we not work hard enough? What are we not doing? Is there some key we are missing?*

We watched as friends started churches at the same time and even after us that would grow immediately. They would need new buildings because of their explosive growth. Why was God blessing them and not us? We moved from depending on God and begging for His help to being angry at Him, then came the hurt, depression, and finally numbness.

During this time, we were in two car accidents within a year of each other. We were rear-ended both times, and both times, our vans were totaled. This all added to our frustration and our confusion. Why was God doing all this? Why was He so obviously not blessing us? Why did He seem to be against us? Unfortunately for us, things were about to go from bad to worse.

Chapter Five

The Night of Our Car Fire

Boom! I sat straight up in bed, my heart thudding in my chest. I didn't know what had woken me. I didn't know what time it was; it was still dark out. We had gone to bed late, exhausted from all the excitement that only comes once a year – Christmas Day. I couldn't find my voice because of the adrenaline coursing through my body. Before I could wake Matt up, I heard banging on the front door. This startled me into action, "Matt, wake up! Something's wrong! Someone's banging on the front door!"

Matt jumped out of bed faster than me. He ran out of the door of our bedroom and into the hallway lead-

the Hidden Pain

ing to the kids' room. I pushed aside my covers and crawled out of bed behind him. As I entered the kids' room, my eyes were drawn to the eerie glow coming from the kids' window.

Just as I noticed it, Matt yelled, "Bob and Debbie's house is on fire!" Bob and Debbie were our neighbors. We shared a driveway with them. A second later, he looked out of the window and exclaimed, "No, it's our van! Our van is on fire!" Those few words pulled me out of the daze I was in and propelled me into action.

"Malachi and Madison, get out of bed – now! There's a fire!" Malachi and Madison woke up and jumped into action. I grabbed Maggie (who was one at the time) out of her crib and flew down the stairs behind Malachi and Madison. Matt dressed lightning fast and followed us down the stairs to the front door where someone was still banging.

I opened the front door and saw the police officer who had been knocking on our door. Beyond him was a confusing mass of neighbors, all yelling and shouting advice at the same time. We walked quickly through the door, and I was hit with a blast of heat. Stunned for just a second, I glanced over at our van, and it was completely engulfed in flames that were shooting high into the sky.

The officer asked, "Is everybody out of the house?" His question brought me back to the moment. "Yes," I quickly answered. Without looking back at the van, I walked down the steps with the kids and followed one of our neighbors to the safety of their home. One of them took Maggie from my arms to carry her for me and told Matt to stay – he would see to it that the kids and I were safe.

As I walked away from our home and burning van in my pajamas, I was in shock. I kept begging God to help the firefighters get there quickly. I begged him to keep my husband and the police officer safe. I knew the danger of the situation. I knew the fire was just a few feet from our electric box and was burning much too close to our home.

I walked into the neighbor's house, and she led us over to her couch to sit down. With a promise to keep me updated, the man passed Maggie back to me and turned to go back and help. Our sweet neighbor put on cartoons for my kids to watch, and nobody said a word. My kids didn't ask any questions. I was glad because I didn't have any answers for them. I put a hand on my pregnant belly to reassure myself that our baby girl was okay. After a moment, I decided to call my mom and inform her what had happened and ask her to pray. I kept listening, but still didn't hear sirens. I couldn't look out of the window because the fear in my heart was too strong.

Glancing at my phone, I saw it was now 3:30 a.m. which meant it was 2:30 a.m. for my mom. My mom groggily answered the phone, "Hello?"

"Mom, I'm so sorry to wake you. I just wanted you to know our van is on fire. Would you please pray that the firefighters will get here soon and that everything will be okay?" The words flowed out of my mouth in a torrent.

"What?" my mom shrieked. She started crying and yelling at me at the same time, "Get out of there! Are you okay? What is going on?"

"Mom, we're okay," I tried to calm her. "It's okay. I'm at a neighbor's house with the kids. We're going to be okay. Just please pray that the fire department gets here soon." With that, I finished quickly, telling her I would keep her informed and hung up.

The Night of Our Car Fire

Then I sat silently in agony. There was absolutely nothing I could do but sit there and pray. I kept begging God for safety and kept straining my ear to hear the sirens.

After what seemed like an eternity but was probably only about twenty minutes, I finally heard them – sirens! Help was on the way. I still couldn't look out of the window. I sat there with my kids, watching some stupid cartoon. Finally about an hour or so later, the neighbor man came back and told us it was safe to go home.

I thanked the neighbor lady, picked up Maggie, and scooted Malachi and Madison out of the door. We walked quietly down the block toward our home and our now-charred van, still in our pajamas and bare feet. There were two fire trucks, the police officer, and several firefighters still on the scene. The firefighters were standing around talking and laughing, but they grew quiet as we got closer. I tried to thank them, but my voice failed me. I managed to mumble, "Thank you," as we walked past them and into the house.

I looked in dismay at the scene before me. The presents from yesterday had been pushed into a pile out of the way. The carpet was covered with black boot marks from the firefighters who had gone inside to check the house and make sure everything was okay. I walked over to the couch and collapsed onto it. By now, it was after 5 a.m. The kids' new Christmas presents lay forgotten on the floor. I asked them if they wanted to go back to bed, but they said no. They were too scared.

Matt came inside and wearily sat down on the couch. Before I had a chance to ask him anything, he pulled out his phone and called his parents. He briefly explained what had happened, then he hung up the phone and said they were on their way to come help us. They lived about an hour away.

Soon a tow truck arrived. The kids and I watched from the window as our charred and broken van was loaded onto the bed of the truck and taken away. A little while later, Matt's parents and sister showed up, full of questions and concern.

They had questions we didn't have answers for. We had just come from their house the night before. What had happened? Was something wrong with the van? Had we been having problems with it? I will never for-

The Night of Our Car Fire

get the feeling deep in the pit of my stomach when my father-in-law, a mechanic by trade, said, "Son, there is no way a van that has been sitting cool for hours can burst into flames like that."

Matt looked at him. "Are you saying that somebody set it on fire on purpose?" Matt asked incredulously.

Matt's dad looked at him and simply said, "I'm not saying that for sure, but it shouldn't have caught fire like that."

Matt looked at me, and I looked at him. I had never considered that possibility. If it was the truth, it meant that somebody had done this on purpose. Without saying anything because the kids were still in the room, Matt and I both instinctively knew that if it was true, we knew who had set it.

I had testified in a court case involving a member from our church just weeks before. A cold knot settled in my stomach as fear settled into my heart.

In the days to come, we would find out from a firefighter and a police detective that the fire was indeed intentionally set by someone.

Unrelenting Fear

The fear that poured into me that night wrapped itself around my heart and began a destructive work in me. I had never been a fearful person before, but everything changed that night. From the moment I looked out the window and knew there was a fire on the other side of the window to the moment I stepped onto my front porch and felt the searing heat and heard the incredibly loud crackling of the fire, to the moment my father-in-law said there is no way the van should have done that, fear began to take hold of my life.

Looking back on that night, I know without a shadow of a doubt that an angel had to be guarding the side of our home. As hot as the fire blazed and as far and as high as the fire was shooting flames, it's a miracle our house was completely unharmed. But even knowing that didn't stop the fear of the "what ifs" from wreaking havoc in my life. What if we hadn't woken up? What if the fire had spread up to the kids' bedroom which was right above where the van was parked? What if we hadn't made it out of the house and the fire had moved inside? A lot of these fears weren't even rational, but that's the problem with fear

The Night of Our Car Fire

– it's not rational.

The night after the fire, I tossed and turned and couldn't sleep all night. My body wanted to sleep, but my mind wouldn't let me. My mind told me I needed to stay awake and alert to protect my family.

Fear Began to Take Control of My Life

Over the course of the next few weeks, fear began to take over my life. Every night, if I did manage to fall asleep, I would wake up like clockwork around 3 a.m. and couldn't go back to sleep. I would wake up with every little noise. I had a hard time walking into my children's bedroom and looking at the window. My mind would jump back to that moment of intense fear when I looked through that very window and saw the fire on the other side.

I convinced Matt to help me change the bedrooms around. We moved our bedroom to the main floor. The bedroom was smaller, but it was closer to the front door. I wanted to be able to hear if someone banged on our door again in the middle of the night.

Fear does crazy things when it takes hold of you. Fear took away my peace. Fear took away my sleep. If you have ever battled fear, you know it for the monster it is. It takes root and gains more and more power while simultaneously weakening you.

I tried to tell a few people what I was going through, but nobody understood. I remember bringing it up to a group of people in our home for a Bible study. I remember one person telling me to just surrender it to God. After that, I decided I couldn't talk to anyone about it. I was a pastor's wife, for goodness sake! I convinced myself that it wasn't that big of a deal. It was just a van. Nobody got hurt. Everything was fine. People have way worse things happen to them all the time! I began shaming myself which just allowed fear to gain an even stronger foothold in my life.

Looking back to that time, I can now see how this only made things worse. Back then, I convinced myself that it wasn't a big deal. I told myself that I should just "get over it." I stuffed down my emotions and didn't talk to anybody about what I was going through. I could deal with it during the day; but when night came, fear would take hold again.

One of the lessons I learned because of this time in my life is not to belittle people's pain and trials.

Everybody deals with different trials and pain. Some seem like a bigger deal than others. We are sometimes tempted to think, *Why are they making such a big deal out of this? That is nothing compared to what I have been through.* We shouldn't do that. Instead, we need to ask God for empathy and compassion for them. Compassion says, "I feel for you. I am sorry for what you are going through." Empathy says, "I am going to place myself in your shoes and allow myself to feel what you are going through and then walk through it with you."

Thankfully, God got me through this season in my life. It took about a year and a half before I finally started sleeping through the night again. Looking back now, there were a few things that got me through that horrible year and a half, one of which was time. Just as in grief, time does heal. I thought I wouldn't get victory over the fear I felt, but slowly over time, it began to fade. As time passed, I didn't wake up as much in the night, and eventually, I finally slept through the night.

Conquering the Fear

One of the habits I developed during that time which

continues today was reading my Bible right before I went to sleep. Even now, the last thing I do before I drift off to sleep is read a chapter from Psalms or Proverbs on my phone before I go to sleep. I also started memorizing Scripture and would quote that to myself before drifting off to sleep. If I woke up during the night, I would again quote Scripture to myself until I could fall back asleep.

I finally learned to talk about what I was going through. It took me a long time, but I finally opened up. The more I brought fear into the light and talked about what I was going through, the more it faded. I wish I wouldn't have waited so long to talk about it. I could have started the healing process sooner, but God was so good to me and helped me get through it. My go-to verse became II Timothy 1:7, "For God hath not given us the spirit of fear; but of power, and of love, and of a sound mind." I begged God to help me have a sound mind. Over time, He restored my mind and helped me conquer the stronghold that fear had on me.

Chapter Six

A Change of Heart

As I was sitting on my bed getting ready to take my contacts out and go to sleep one night, Matt walked into our bedroom and tossed a book on my lap. I looked up at him questioningly.

"I bought that for you today. It's by some lady who has a blog or something. I thought you might like it." That was it. It was such a simple gesture, but in the days to come, it would have huge ramifications.

I picked up the book and looked at it. It was called Money Saving Mom by Crystal Paine. I turned the book over and looked at the back. It gave a short description of the book and described the author as a blogger.

"What's a blogger?" I looked up and asked Matt.

"It's somebody who writes articles online or something like that," he replied.

"Hmm. It looks interesting," I replied. Then I placed the book on the floor next to my bed and went to sleep.

I think it was a few days before I picked that book up again and read it. Once I started, I didn't want to put it down. I've been an avid reader all my life, but fiction was usually my reading of choice. I had never really gotten into non-fiction books because they were boring, or so I thought.

As I read Crystal's book, it was as if she was talking directly to me. I could relate to her story, and reading her book started stirring something inside of me. Reading her book opened up an entirely new world to me—the world of blogging. Something inside of me clicked. I wasn't sure how it was going to all come together, but I began to feel like blogging might be something God had for me.

I cruised through Money Saving Mom, and a few days later, Matt surprised me with two more new books. These books were both by Lysa TerKeurst – one was called The Bathtub is Overflowing but I Feel Drained, and the second was titled Am I Messing Up My Kids? … and Other Questions Moms Ask. These books both read like fiction. Every chapter started with a story, and the author was hilarious! Her stories were similar to mine, and I could so relate. I would be laughing one minute and then crying the next. I read every book she wrote and began to follow her blog.

Sometime later, Crystal Paine's second book, Say Goodbye to Survival Mode, was released. I read it cover to cover and loved it! It was exactly what I needed. Eventually, Crystal's third book, Money-Making Mom, came out and pushed me further in the direction of wanting to start a business of my own.

God used these two women, both of whom I have yet to meet, in an incredible way in my life. During a time of deep discouragement and loneliness for me, they became the mentors I didn't have. Through their books and blogs, they encouraged my weary heart. It was because of them that I decided to blog and eventually write. I wanted to be able to help women through my writing the same way they helped me through their books.

It wasn't until several years later that it came to fruition and my blog, Faithfully Stepping, was born. My love of blogging as well as my desire to help encourage ladies on their journey of faith can be traced back to Crystal Paine, Lysa TerKeurst, and the simple act of kindness Matt showed by buying a few books for me.

Reading those books changed everything for me. Now that I had been exposed to really good, entertaining, non-fiction books, I was hooked. I became a voracious reader. Around the same time, Matt found a few really good books on church planting, and he became hooked on reading as well. We began reading anything and everything. We read church growth books, leadership books, encouraging and uplifting books, statistic books, business books, discipline books, and anything else we could get our hands on.

Getting Outside of Ourselves

As we started meeting new authors through the books we were reading, our world began to open up. We began to see different ministries using different methods, other churches doing things in new ways, different businesses being successful, and so much more. We discovered new blogs and books and podcasts. We started listening to podcasts constantly.

We began to change as individuals and as a pastor and pastor's wife. God began to change us. Matt took preaching classes, public speaking courses, and more. We began to work harder than ever but on ourselves, not the church. God began to get ahold of our hearts, and He began to change us.

Continuing to Grow

We began to understand that if we were going to stay faithful in the work God called us to do, we needed to constantly grow. There are so many verses in the Bible about growing in our faith, in our relationship to God, and as a person.

> But grow in grace, and in the knowledge of our Lord and Savior Jesus Christ. To him be glory both now and forever. (II Peter 3:18)

> But speaking the truth in love, may

> grow up into him in all things, which is the head, even Christ. (Ephesians 4:15)
>
> As newborn babes, desire the sincere milk of the word, that ye may grow thereby. (I Peter 2:2)
>
> We are bound to thank God always for you, brethren, as it is meet, because that your faith groweth exceedingly, and the charity of every one of you all toward each other aboundeth. (II Thessalonians 1:3)

God doesn't want us to stop reading and learning and growing simply because we grow into adults, start families, and move on with life. He wants us to continue to develop our minds, our abilities and talents, and our personalities. What He wants more than that, however, is for us to develop our relationship with Him. He wants us to continue to work at our relationship with Him.

How can we do that? We can grow in our relationship with God by faithfully attending church, getting involved in a Bible study or small group, and spending time each day reading our Bibles, praying, and journaling.

I am passionate about Bible reading, praying, and journaling. I believe it is the best way to develop our relationship with God. Spending time each day connecting with God is the surest way to develop a relationship with Him.

Developing a Relationship

I remember when I moved from Illinois to Pennsylvania when Matt and I first got married. I didn't know anybody except Matt's family. Matt and I hadn't been working at the church for very long, and we didn't know many people. But we knew we needed to make friends if we were going to stay encouraged, so we decided to start inviting couples into our home.

I remember the first time we had a young couple over who were about our age. We welcomed them into our small apartment. That night was so awkward. We didn't really know them, and they didn't really know us. We had almost nothing in common. He was a roofer; Matt was interning to be a pastor. She taught special education in public school; I taught kindergarten in a Christian school.

We tried to make small talk. Well ... Matt did. He's more of a talker than I am in new situations. I'm pretty sure they said about two words the entire time they were at our house. The man didn't eat anything on his plate; his wife managed to swallow a few bites. I was mortified. It was such a horrible night. I didn't relax until they left and we shut the door behind them. I was sure we would never hang out with them again.

God had different plans. It wasn't too long before Matt talked me into meeting with them again. Soon they invited us to their house for a game night. Twelve years of friendship, countless dinners, game nights, and eleven kids later, they are some of our closest friends. We have walked through so much together. We have laughed together, cried together, and gone through the ups and downs of life together. How did we go from awkward and weird to a close friendship? Time. We chose to spend time together. We chose to get to know each other and to understand what makes us laugh and cry, what moves us, and what frustrates us. We chose to keep spending time together. Every time we spent time together, our hearts knit closer to each other.

This is exactly how we grow in our relationship with God. It's not mystical and magical. If we want to develop a relationship with God, we simply must choose to spend time with Him. We find out what He likes and doesn't like, what frustrates Him, and what delights Him. We do this by setting time aside each day to spend with Him.

For me, this happens first thing in the morning. I light a candle, make a cup of coffee, grab my morning-time basket, and begin my time with God. I pray, read my Bible, and journal. I have written a book about this called Better Mornings, Better Moms. You can download a free copy by going to my blog, Faithfullystepping.com. I am passionate about helping women connect to Jesus through an effective morning time routine. It's the most important part of our day as Christian women.

My morning routine is the foundation of my life. I know without a doubt that I would have walked away from everything by now if I hadn't developed a habit of spending time with God every single morning. I live for my mornings!

Chapter Seven

Change and Criticism

With our newfound love of reading, Matt and I began growing as a couple and as individuals. As we did, we finally started gaining some perspective. It was as if we had come out from under a rock and were looking around at a whole new world. We started wrapping our minds around what God was doing in our lives and ministry.

We began to realize we were putting things on God that we shouldn't have. I guess some time over the last several years, we subconsciously shifted into this mindset that God owed us. We began to put expectations on God that He never agreed to. God didn't

the Hidden Pain

promise us a big church. God didn't promise us success. He didn't promise things would be easy. He promised His presence. God simply asked us to obey Him. Whether or not the church was a success was totally up to Him. We began to better understand I Peter 5:10, "But the God of all grace, who hath called us unto his eternal glory by Christ Jesus, after that ye have suffered a while, make you perfect, stablish, strengthen, settle you."

The best way I can describe it is that we finally started to settle. We finally began to find strength in being who God created us to be. We could stop trying so hard. He began to show us a better way than just being busy 24/7. God worked in our hearts to show us that our worth was not wrapped up in our work.

We started changing the way we ran our ministry. We began pulling back. We realized that all of our busyness wasn't really accomplishing anything. We began to cut all of the extra programs we had going at church. People weren't coming anyway, so why go crazy pushing ourselves so hard? We started to realize that our plans were not God's plans, and His timing was not our timing. We were ready for God to grow the church and for Him to do it NOW! However, that wasn't His plan. I don't know why; I wish I did.

Moses' Example

One of the Biblical examples we encouraged ourselves with so often during this season of life was the story of Moses. Moses is a fascinating character to study. Most people know that Moses' story is found in the Old Testament, but most people don't know that Moses' name is mentioned 79 times in the New Testament too.

Moses is most well-known for leading over a million people out of captivity in Egypt. He led the children of Israel in the wilderness for 40 long years. For 40 years, he was responsible for this enormous group of people, God's chosen people. Yet Moses makes an appearance in the New Testament too. Moses appeared on the Mount of Transfiguration with Jesus Christ. Of all the amazing forerunners to Christ, Moses is one of two people who come to Jesus on the mountain.

What I find most fascinating is that God spent 80 years preparing Moses for a 40-year ministry. He was in training longer than he was in battle. It was good Moses didn't know this ahead of time, or he may have been tempted to skip a few years of training. It took 80 years for God to determine that Moses was fit and ready to do the task He called him to – 80 years! That is an entire lifetime for us! God was taking Moses deep.

Why did I think that prepping for a few years in Bible college would prepare me enough for God to use me in a great way? Could it be that God was taking me deeper? Taking us deeper? Could it be that the deeper the ministry and impact, the longer and more intensive the training would be?

There were several churches that started around the same time we started our church. Matt and I would look at Facebook and Twitter and see the amazing quick growth they were having, and we would get so discouraged, especially on Sunday nights which continued until I banned Twitter on Sunday nights. (This is a really good practice if your husband is a pastor because everybody posts their Sunday service stats on Twitter on Sunday nights.)

Anyway, if we would have had the quick success many other churches had, I don't know that it would have been good for us. It would have been much less painful; that's for certain! But I don't know that we

Change and Criticism

would have read and grown as much as we have over the last several years if we had experienced early success in our church planting efforts. I know with one hundred percent certainty that Matt and I are not the same people we were when we started the church. We have changed and grown so much.

As with any change, along with that change came criticism. It started small. People began asking why we were doing this or not doing that. Why did we change this? Why did we cancel that ministry? The more we changed, the harsher the criticism. The criticism came hard, and it came fast. The thing about change and the criticism that accompanies it is that it actually works in your favor. People don't realize this when they criticize you for doing what you are doing or being who you were created to be instead of who they *want* you to be. Their criticism either crumbles you or makes you stronger. The more the criticism comes, the stronger you stand because the criticism actually solidifies in your mind that you are doing the right thing.

I would love to say that Matt and I took the criticism easily and didn't let it get to us, but that wouldn't be true. It hurt ... a lot. Eventually though, we began to get used to it. We chose to keep our heads down and continue in what we knew God had for us and our ministry. A verse I constantly went back to and continue to remind myself of is found in I Corinthians 4:3,4, "But with me it is a very small thing that I should be judged of you, or of man's judgment: yea, I judge not mine own self. For I know nothing by myself; yet am I not hereby justified: but he that judgeth me is the Lord."

We had to constantly remind ourselves and each other that we are not out to please people and get their approval. Our approval comes from God. This concept freed us to do what we needed to do and change what we needed to change to move forward. Because we understood that only God is our judge, we were able to move forward without constant fear of our critics.

Chapter Eight

I Don't Owe an Explanation

"So, how's the church going?" asked a sweet person who didn't attend our church.

Aw! It's the dreaded question – the one that always hits a nerve. It's the one question that makes me want to lie in response to it, more so than any other question I ever get. Whenever we are making polite conversation, inevitably somebody always asks how the church is going. On the surface, it sounds like a really good question. Usually though, there is another question that follows right on the heels of the first question, "How many people are you running?"

That one question has so much power behind it!

the Hidden Pain

It's a question that has an answer that has haunted me for several years. You see, in the "church business," numbers are success. The more numbers (aka people in your church), the more of a success you considered to be. The opposite is also true. The fewer people you have in your church, the more of a failure you are. I'm not saying that's the truth, or that it's even a good system. I'm just saying that's how the system works.

For the first five years of our ministry, I would have considerable angst over my answer to that question. I would respond with how many we had recently had in church, followed by an explanation of any good momentum we had going, and anything else positive I could add to make ourselves look more successful than we really were. I mean, let's face it – five adults in your Sunday morning service is not something you can exaggerate and make sound good.

Letting People Have Power Over Us

It's amazing how much power we let other people have over us, isn't it? Somebody poses a question, and we immediately launch into protection or proving mode. Either we protect ourselves from the inevitable judgment we feel is coming, or we strive to prove that our way, theory, or idea is the best. I have had conversations with ladies that can start with an innocent question such as, "What do you get your picky toddler to eat for breakfast?" Suddenly, it becomes a heated debate over which brand and type of cereal we believe is best as if we were representatives of that cereal company, trying to prove that it's the best one! It's ridiculous! We get so prideful or insecure that we can't even carry on a normal conversation without defending or proving ourselves. Neither pride nor insecurity is good. Neither wins any friends.

Pride pushes people away because you always dominate the conversation and your opinion is *always* the right one. Insecurity keeps you from even giving your opinion, and thereby, people glide right over you in the conversation. This is all brought on because of shame. We are too busy shaming one another when we should be offering grace. In her book, *Present over Perfect,* Shauna Niequist says, "For so many of us, what religion taught us was how to feel ashamed. For many years, my spiritual life was one more place to measure up and be found wanting. It is only when you understand God's truly unconditional love that you begin to understand the worth of your own soul—not because of anything you've done, but because every soul is worthy, every one of us is worthy of love having been created by and in the image of the God of love."[2]

I am trying to learn that when people ask a question, it's just that—a question. I don't need to take it personally. I don't need to defend myself or prove my worth. I now respond with how many we recently had in church, then I stop. I don't continue with excuses or conversation fillers to make myself feel better. I just stop with the actual answer to the question.

Even if it's a loaded question, I still answer and move on to a safer topic. I don't have to explain myself to everyone I run into. It was so freeing when I finally started getting the hang of that! I can run into someone and not panic and want to run for the door. I can stick around long enough to make polite conversation, but I don't have to tell them every detail of my life. I don't owe anybody any explanations. Now sometimes, people ask because they truly want to know, and I feel safe talking to them. I can open up to them without having to prove anything or defend myself.

Genuine Success

I can talk until I am blue in the face, but the person I am talking to probably already has an idea in mind of what success looks like to them. Chances are, it doesn't look like my definition. As I started freeing myself from getting into those kinds of dangerous conversations, it started me thinking, *What is true success anyway? What does it look like in God's eyes? What does it look like in my life? What does it look like in the Bible?*

Eugene Peterson, author of *The Message*, defines success as "long obedience in the same direction." I love that quote! The word *success* is only mentioned one time in the Bible, and it's found in the Old Testament. Joshua 1:8 says, "This book of the law shall not depart out of thy mouth; but thou shalt meditate therein day and night, that thou mayest observe to do according to all that is written therein: for then thou shalt make thy way prosperous, and then thou shalt have good **success**."

God was preparing Joshua to be the leader of the great nation of Israel because Moses had died. Joshua was no stranger to leadership. He worked under Moses, commanding the army and leading the Israelites into battle repeatedly. Now it was time for him to take the next step. God was preparing him to be an incredible leader. God told him that the best way to be prosperous and successful was simply to know God's Word, think on it, and obey it.

What does any of that have to do with leading a million-strong group of God's people across the dessert and into battle time and time again until they entered the promised land? It's crazy, but God was telling this battle general that if he wanted to be a success, he had to know what real success was. Real success is knowing what the Scriptures say and applying them to your life.

Jesus' Teaching

Around 1400 years later, Jesus came onto the scene and further added to this teaching.

> In the beginning was the word, and the word was with God, and the word was God. (John 1:1)

> The word became flesh and made his dwelling among us. We have seen his

> glory, the glory of the one and only,
> who came from the Father, full of grace
> and truth. (John 1:14)

Revelation also records the correlation of the Word of God being God.

> He is dressed in a robe dipped in blood, and his name is the word of God. (Revelation 19:13)

If we take the principle God was teaching Joshua – that to know the Scripture and to obey it would bring success – and add to it what Jesus taught in the New Testament – that Jesus was the Word of God, here is what we get … **true success comes from knowing Jesus and obeying Him.** It's as simple as that!

A couple thousand years later, this teaching still applies to us today. God says that if we want to be successful, we have to get to know Him. How can we do that? By studying His Word and developing a personal relationship with Him.

What True Success Looks Like

Over time as God started to change my perspective, He has opened my eyes to what success looks like for me. I am a success in life but not because I have accomplished anything great with my life. No, I am a success because I have learned how to cultivate a real relationship with the Lord. I begin almost every day by spending time with Him.

Through the years, I have developed a morning-time routine that works for me. I use a specific journaling system that has worked for me for years. When I do this, it doesn't matter how the rest of my day goes. I know I got the most important part of my day in. I am growing in my relationship with God every day. So if others don't approve of me or don't see me as a success, that's okay. I know the truth. God calls me a success! That's way better than what anybody else can say about me!

I love this quote from the book *Wild and Free: A Hope-Filled Anthem for the Woman Who Feels She is Both Too Much and Never Enough* by Jess Connolly and Hayley Morgan, "When a woman knows she is completely and utterly free, she doesn't fear the opinions of others, doesn't fear failing, and doesn't stay up late worrying about the details. She walks though her days knowing she is free indeed."[3] I want that to be me.

Chapter Nine

Starting
Faithfully Stepping

Early one morning, I was reading a book called *Life-Giving Leadership* by Julia Mateer. I had just finished reading my Bible and journaling and was sipping on a cup of coffee reading her book when a sentence flew off the page at me. She wrote, "Turning your pain into ministry enables you to move forward in life so that you are not defined by adversity. The extent to which you allow God to heal you is the extent to which you will be able to help others."[4] I put down my cup of coffee, read it again, then grabbed my pen, and underlined it. I turned that over in my mind for a few minutes. I kept reading. A few pages later I read,

"Our messes become our ministries. Our messes also make us relatable and relevant."[5]

How could I use my pain to help others? What did that look like for me? At first, it seemed like a foolish idea. So many people have gone through such heartache. What was my pain compared to someone going through cancer or losing a loved one? I went back to reading my book, but I couldn't get that thought out of my mind. I thought about it often in the following days. I thought about the fact that our trial has been an ongoing, several-year-long trial, and I have learned so many lessons during this time. Maybe I could help someone else who is going through something similar. I definitely didn't want to waste the pain of what I had gone through. What was the point in learning lessons and being taught so much if I had no one to share it with?

I didn't know what God wanted me to do, but I knew He was working in my heart. Sometimes God asks us to take a giant leap. Now it may not seem like a giant leap by anyone else's standards, but it is by our standards. That is how my blog got started. I really felt God wanted me to start a blog, but it never seemed to come together. For almost two years, I read books on blogging, took notes, and listened to podcasts, but I never really knew what I could blog about. I don't really have any special hobbies or talents.

I wasn't super passionate about anything in particular besides my life with my husband and kids and our church. Nothing really jumped out at me. I spent hours and days and weeks agonizing over what to blog. I had to at least have a title and a direction to get started.

Faithfully Stepping

Finally, I knew I had to do something. God just kept burdening my heart, and our finances kept getting tighter and tighter. I knew I had to take the plunge. As I was listening to a sermon one day, the words "stepping faithfully" jumped out at me. I told God I would use that phrase and start my blog. There was only one problem – we had no money. I waited another week, and we still had no extra money. I kept begging God for extra money to start my blog. Not only did we not receive any extra money; but the week I started my blog, I had to order home-school curriculum, buy groceries for our extended family for a week at the beach, and pay for a new car battery for our van. Circumstances were certainly against me. It was the absolute worst time to "blow" money on starting a blog, yet deep in my heart, I knew God wanted me to do it and He wanted me to do it now. So, I used the very little money we had in our bank account to start my blog.

I stepped out completely in faith, knowing it was up to God to catch me in my free fall. Appropriately, I decided to call it *Faithfully Stepping*. If there was only one lesson I learned over the last several years of testing, it was that I had to choose each day to have faith that God was still working in my life. I just need to faithfully step into what He has for me each day and leave the rest to Him.

As I started blogging, I was finally able to find joy again. I don't mean that I always walked around "happy." I still had hard days—still *have* hard days. I still get really discouraged, and at times, I still feel as though God is not for me.

Not every day is a happy day. But after several long years, I feel like I am getting to the place where I can still have joy no matter the circumstances. One thing about failing at what you are doing for such long time is that you are able to ride out the ups and downs a little better. You realize your emotions don't have to be tied to your circumstances. Today may not be a good day to be happy, but it is a good day to have joy.

When you get to a place where you are not ruled by the sadness you feel, you begin to see that you can thrive even though you are still enduring your trial. For us personally, our circumstances haven't changed. We are still under an incredible amount of pressure and financial strain. Before, we would have been miserable. Now, we still feel the pressure, but we hand it over to God and continue on with life. One of my favorite verses is a small verse found in the book of I Peter 5:7, "Casting all your care upon him; for he careth for you."

I so often forget to take this verse at face value. I need to remember that God never meant for me to carry my own burdens! He wants to carry them for me.

The Weary Backpacker

A story has been told about a young man who was hitchhiking. He walked for several miles with a heavy

the Hidden Pain

backpack on his shoulders. The backpack contained all he owned in the world. It wasn't much, but it was his. After several days of walking and hitching a ride here and there, he was dusty, tired, and weary from the weight of his backpack. As he trudged along, a small white pickup truck pulled slowly alongside him. A kind, older man leaned toward the passenger side door and asked through the open window, "Can I give you a ride?"

"Sure," the weary traveler answered, "That would be awesome."

"Well, throw your backpack in the back and get on in here, boy," the kind man replied.

The young man climbed into the truck without throwing his backpack in the back of the truck. The older man noticed but wisely didn't comment. He noticed that the young man didn't even take the backpack off. He kept it on his back and buckled his seatbelt. It was as if he had carried the backpack for so long that it had become a part of him.

Several miles down the road, the older man couldn't keep quiet anymore. "Son, why don't you take your backpack off? You have to be weary. Why not give those shoulders a break?"

The young man glanced over at the older man, "You don't understand. I can't take it off. This backpack is my burden to carry. It contains all I have left in this world. If I put it down, I might forget it or lose it. Something bad might happen to it. I have to continue carrying it." His voice trailed off, and he gazed out the window.

The wise old man was quiet for a few minutes then responded to the young man, "I understand now that it is very valuable to you and close to your heart, but I also understand how weary you are carrying it. Why don't you trust me to carry your load? Nothing will happen to your bag. I will watch over it. While you are here with me in my truck, why don't you take it off and let the truck carry it for you? Soon enough, you'll arrive at your destination and can put it back on. I'll see to it that it stays safe. You can even rest once you've taken it off. Then you will be more refreshed when it's time to continue on with your journey."

The young man pondered the older man's words. He *was* tired and so weary from carrying his heavy load. It would be wonderful to drop the bag just for a little while and be able to rest. After a moment of indecision, he finally began to wrestle the bag off his shoulders. He placed it carefully at his feet and then sat back against the seat, enjoying the ease in his shoulders. He gazed out the window for just few moments before succumbing to much-needed sleep. The old man shook his head, chuckled to himself quietly, and continued driving.

Carrying Our Burdens

How many of us are just like that young man? We trudge through life with the heavy burdens we are carrying. God offers to take our burdens and carry them for us, but we decline his offer. We feel much more in control if we continue to carry the weight of our burdens ourselves, yet God never designed us to carry heavy burdens. He wants us to give them to Him to carry, but first we have to trust Him. We have to surrender our precious burden to Him, and that can be hard. It's so much easier to worry about my finances, try to figure out what we are going to do, work on getting more income, and stress about it all instead of saying, "Okay, God. Our finances are really messed up right now. I don't know how it's all going to work out, but I give the burden to You. Please work it all out for us and provide for us." That's so hard to do!

Playing God

We need to stop planning, scheming, and trying to play God in our lives and just let Him be God. He's so much better at it than we are! I wonder how many times God just shakes His head and chuckles to Himself at our stupidity in trying to carry our own burdens when the God of the universe is standing right next to us!

When we come to the end of ourselves and ask God to carry our burdens for us, we will realize that is what He intended all along. Once we surrender our burdens and weaknesses to Him, He takes them and then does an amazing thing. He turns around and gives us strength. "And he said unto me, My grace is sufficient for thee: for my strength is made perfect in weakness. Most gladly therefore will I rather glory in my infirmities, that the power of Christ may rest upon me. Therefore I take pleasure in infirmities, in reproaches, in necessities, in persecutions, in distresses for Christ's sake: for when I am weak, then am I strong." II Corinthians 12:9,10

When we have nothing left and we are at our weakest, that's when God does His greatest work. He steps into our weakness and makes us strong, but He can only do this when we surrender our pressures, burdens, hopes, and dreams to Him.

Chapter Ten

God is Still Molding Us

I sat across from Matt at dinner one night. It was our weekly date night, and we had been waiting all day to get the kids dropped off at his parents so we could talk. That day, a church family informed us they were leaving the church. There were no hard feelings. They were moving, and the commute would be too far away to attend our church. For us, however, the blow couldn't have come at a worse time.

We had spent time in prayer, asking God to provide for us. This was not the answer we were looking for. Instead of provision, we were now down another family who were regular givers to the church.

the Hidden Pain

Do you ever feel like sometimes life keeps coming at you and you can't make sense of it? That's how we felt right then. We were praying for God to do something specific, and He did the exact opposite. How do you reconcile that? Sometimes it feels like a slap in the face, and that's how we felt that night – hurt, tired, discouraged, and unsure of what to do next.

We have experienced years of feeling as if we don't have God's blessing. If you have experienced that, you know what a hard thing it is. It's hard because you have faith that God can meet your deepest need, but for some reason, He is choosing not to. For us, God could grow our church exponentially and bring around the finances we need in just a few weeks, but He hasn't chosen to do that.

Sometimes I think that having faith is harder than not having faith. When you have faith, you know God *can* meet your every need and provide. You totally believe that, so then when it doesn't happen, you feel even more discouraged. Because you know He is able to, if it doesn't happen, you know that He is actively choosing not to. In her book, *Uninvited,* Lysa TerKeurst says, "My head long ago nodded a big yes to His existence. It's because I know He exists and I know He loves me that things get so confusing and complicated. My heart struggles to make peace between God's ability to change hard things and His apparent decision not to change them for me."[6] That is true and so difficult. If I'm not careful, I slip into "victim" mode.

When I play the victim, the focus is on me. Now don't get me wrong, it is important to talk about how you feel and process what's going on. It's okay to ask God questions and talk to Him about my frustrations, but I can't move forward and claim victory until I stop playing the victim. Contrary to how it feels, everybody is not out to get me, God still loves me, and everything will eventually be okay.

God's Not Done

I recently heard a pastor say, "If it's not all good, God's not all done." If you are doing your best to love God and follow His plan for your life but things are just not working out, then God's not all done. There is more He is trying to do. He is trying to strip away everything that stands in the way of making you who He wants you to be. He sees the finished you – the completed you. He is going to do everything in His power to keep molding you, breaking you, reforming you, and changing you until you are the person He wants you to become.

Joseph's Example

I wonder if this is how Joseph from the Old Testament felt. I feel for him. Every time it seemed as though his life was going okay, everything would fall apart. When he was young, his brothers resented him. This must have hurt him. Sometimes it's hard to see Biblical characters as we see ourselves today, but we need to try to put ourselves in his shoes. From an early age, kids know who the favorites are, just like Joseph and his brothers did.

One night I was putting our kids to bed, and Madison, who was six at the time, asked me, "Mom, who do you like the most? Malachi, Maggie, Macey, or me?" I was totally shocked that she asked me that. As a parent, you think you are so good at being neutral, but apparently I was not. I went on to explain to her that I don't have a favorite child. I love them all just the same!

Joseph must have felt the pain of being rejected by his brothers. Sure, his dad loved him the most, but his brothers all hated him. Sounds like a lose-lose situation to me. Then Joseph received an exquisite gift from his dad. He received a beautiful and valuable coat. So maybe for a little bit, it felt worth it. For just a few minutes, it was worth it to be the most favored child.

But just hours later, that same coat landed him in a mess, specifically in a pit. Then his brothers sold him as a slave. His brothers hated him so much that they sold him to a caravan of strangers traveling to Egypt.

In Egypt, he was sold to a man named Potiphar. Potiphar lived a life of prominence. As time passed, Joseph proved himself valuable and a man of integrity. Before long, Joseph became the head of Potiphar's entire household. Things really turned around for Joseph, but as soon as things were getting better, the bottom dropped out. Potiphar's wife wrongly accused Joseph, and Joseph found himself in prison.

As I said before, every time Joseph's life seemed to start going well, everything would fall apart. Once inside the prison, Joseph began to move up the ranks, just as he had done in Potiphar's home. Soon the guards began to see the integrity and character in Joseph. It wasn't long before Joseph was entrusted with being an overseer of the other prisoners. After a few years, Joseph was given the opportunity to stand before Pharaoh and interpret his dream. After that, Joseph moved into a position of incredible authority. He was second in command of all of Egypt.

We look at Joseph's life and say, "See, it all worked out in the end!" But how long did it take? Joseph was only seventeen years old when he was sold into slavery, and it wasn't until the age of thirty that he became second in command in Egypt. That's thirteen years! How long does it take somebody to be ready for God to use them? How many trials and tests does it take before God blesses them? For Joseph, it was thirteen years.

God's Molding of Us

How long has it been for you? Is God still in the process of molding you and changing you? He still is for me, and it's painful. I feel like I have been broken so many times. I feel He just keeps hammering away at me, but I know He has a plan. He's trying to get rid of that anger that so often rears itself in this mama ... He is trying to eradicate the pride that stands out so strongly in my life ... He is trying to build a boldness for Him in this shy person ... He is working to toughen me up a little bit so that I am not so sensitive to every little thing people say or do. He has so much work to do in me! Sometimes, it's quite discouraging, but my consolation is realizing that because the tests and trials keep coming, it means God hasn't given up on me. He has a plan for my life! He believes I am valuable to Him and His work; He just needs to develop me more. So, I wait and allow God to keep working, to keep changing me, to keep testing and trying me, and to keep transforming me. Why? Because He values the trying of my faith more valuable than gold. "That the trial of your faith, being much more precious than of gold that perisheth, though it be tried with fire, might be found unto praise and honour and glory at the appearing of Jesus Christ." I Peter 1:7

I find huge encouragement in the words I read in *Uninvited* by Lysa TerKeurst, "Hold fast to Jesus and remember: This breaking of you will be the making of you. A new you. A stronger you. Strengthened not with the pride of perfection but with the sweet grace of one who knows an intimate closeness with her Lord."[7]

Chapter Eleven

The Bottom Drops Out

You know when you read a book and you keep waiting for the pivotal circumstance to happen? You know, that event that changes the trajectory of the story? Well, our pivotal circumstance took place around year seven of our church plant. It changed the trajectory of our story, but probably not in the way you might think.

We were plugging along, struggling really. We couldn't get any momentum, then the bottom fell out. After we lost that first giving family, we lost two more only a few months later. All three families moved away. While we were happy for them and their new

the Hidden Pain

opportunities, we were devastated.

We started praying and fasting more than we ever had in the last seven years. We knew that without a miracle from God, we wouldn't be able to sustain the church. We were in serious trouble.

Six months prior to losing these families, Matt began writing a book. He had spent hours and hours writing it and proofreading it. We then handed it off to a professional editor. We spent the next several weeks making revisions and working with the editor. We were moving toward releasing it on Amazon. Well, it just so happened that the same week the last of the three families moved away was the same week Matt's book was slated to come out. Our friends said goodbye on Sunday, and Matt's book came out on Tuesday.

As we moved toward the book launch date, we were sick with worry and fear. We knew God would take care of us, but there was so much at stake. We already knew we wouldn't be receiving a paycheck that month. There wasn't enough money in the church account to clear it. There was barely enough money to pay the bills for the church. We had a mortgage to pay, insurance, all our bills, and food and gas to provide for our family ... and there was no check coming. Matt and I begged God and fasted and prayed.

I remember Matt telling me, "We are at the Red Sea. The Egyptians are closing in behind us, and the Red Sea is before us. The only thing that can save us is a miracle from God." During that same time, I read a verse in Psalms that became our go-to phrase. It was Psalm 119:26, "It is time for thee, Lord, to work." We prayed this verse so many times and encouraged each other with it.

The pressure on Matt was huge! We couldn't tell people how important this book launch was. The only people who really knew were family members and a few close friends. We launched the book on Amazon for the first three days as a free download. We had a total of 325 downloads. It was much lower than what we were hoping for, but then, after the free days were over ... nothing. Not one book sale. I remember what happened next. I remember the day very clearly.

I Was Done

It was the day I was done. I got up, took a shower, and prepared to leave the house. I didn't read my Bible and

the Hidden Pain

journal, I didn't homeschool my kids, and I didn't fix anybody breakfast. I was numb, and I was done. All of the promises and excitement of what could happen were gone. I had no more hope. The hope that God would come through was gone. We had no paycheck coming. We had sunk every last little bit of money we had into the book, and it was all for naught. I was so discouraged and depressed. I didn't want to talk to my kids. I didn't want to talk to Matt. I only wanted to get out of the house and go somewhere. I wasn't sure where, but I would figure that out when I got in the car.

Before I could leave, Matt stopped me. He wouldn't let me leave without talking to him. I listened while he droned on and on about how God was good and everything was going to be okay. He used my own words against me about God's faithfulness and goodness ... the very same words I had used countless times before. I was in a foul mood and didn't want to be comforted. I just wanted to get away. At one point, he got angry with me and said, "You act like you have no hope! If we have lost hope, then we've got nothing!" He turned and walked away.

"Exactly!" I said to myself quietly. *That's exactly the problem*, I thought to myself. We had been at this for seven years! For seven years I have told myself, *Just wait a little bit longer. This Sunday will be different. We will have more people. This next month will be different; we will have more money. This next year will be better. The church will take off, and we will have enough money to meet our needs.* On and on it went. Seven years. How long was I supposed to hold on to hope? I was pretty sure seven years had to be the max!

Biology says that we can last about three weeks without food and three days without water, but we can't last a moment without hope. If you lose hope, you have lost everything. That's where I was.

The Downward Spiral

Our lives spiraled crazily over the next several months. We went several months without getting paid. With absolutely no money coming in, the bills began piling up. Our credit card maxed out, we had to switch our insurance to Medicaid, and we became eligible for food stamps. Life quickly spiraled seemingly out of control.

the Hidden Pain

Matt started driving for Uber Eats while he waited to get approved to work for Amazon Flex delivering packages. Once Matt got hired at Amazon, we decided it would be easier for us to work the routes together. He drove, and I would jump out and deliver the packages. We would get up early every day, start school, pack sack lunches, then drive an hour away to the Amazon warehouse. While we waited in the long line to load up our packages, the kids would finish their schoolwork in the van. We loaded packages from floor to ceiling around the kids and begin our route for the day. We did this for a few months. It was insanely crazy! You should have seen the looks on the faces of the workers in the warehouse when we pulled up in our family van with four kids inside!

Finally, after cutting all sorts of expenses and making changes, we started receiving a paycheck again. It was half of what it used to be. By this point, our finances were devastated, and we were drowning financially. We knew we had to something, so that year around Christmas time, we sat down at a Starbucks on date night to decide what to do.

The Decision to Move

Matt and I talked for hours. We wrote down pros and cons of staying, leaving, and more. We finally decided to sell our home and move into a smaller home in a different city, so we could bring our mortgage down. That was the decision we both agreed on; but in the back of my mind, I was hesitant.

I knew that if we sold our home and bought a new home, we were committing to stay at Greater Philly Church. We couldn't purchase a house and then move right away. I knew this move would lock us into staying at the church, and I wasn't sure how I felt about that. I knew we had to do something though. I agreed to move forward and contact a realtor. I told God that if He wanted us to stay, He would have to make this whole process move quickly. In the back of my mind, I hung on to the fact that maybe it wouldn't work out.

We made the call to a realtor friend of ours a few days after the new year began. From there, everything flew forward. On February 16th of that year, we held our first open house. Two days later, the house sold. We watched as God knocked down all the barriers and practically threw us into our next home. We moved into our new home the second week of April.

It was a twin, built in the 1950s. It was smaller than our last house and obviously connected, whereas our other home had been a stand-alone house. It had no driveway like our last home. It had one bathroom instead of two, and it didn't have central air like our last place did. However, it had two major things going for it. It was less than ten minutes away from our church, and the mortgage was half of what we paid at the last house.

I remember moving in. As I lay in bed the first night in our new home, I stared at the ceiling. I had a conversation with God that went something like this, "Well, You did it. You brought us through this crazy process. I said that if this worked out, I would take it as my sign from You that we are supposed to stay at the church, so that's what we will do."

With that, some of the pressure and burdens I had been carrying slipped away. I knew that God wanted us to stay, and He would provide for us. God began healing my broken heart. My faith started returning, and my days no longer felt like I was just trying to survive. Everything wasn't perfect, but we would be okay. We finally found footing in our new normal.

the Hidden Pain

Chapter Twelve

Wrestling with God

These last few years have felt like I have been continuously wrestling with God. Have you ever felt like you have wrestled with God? I have, but it's taken me until just recently to justify calling it that. I was listening to Priscilla Shirer on a podcast one afternoon. Priscilla Shirer is a movie actress in *War Room, I Can Only Imagine,* and *Overcomer* and the author of several books and Bible studies. On her podcast, she was talking about Jacob from the book of Genesis and his wrestling match with an angel. She shared that she felt like she has wrestled with God at times. In that moment, I realized that's what has been going on in my life. For the first several years of our struggle, I just kept my head down and kept plodding forward. For these past few years though, I have been actively engaged in wrestling with God. Genesis 32 tells the story of Jacob wrestling with God:

> *And Jacob was left alone; and there wrestled a man with him until the breaking of the day. And when he saw that he prevailed not against him, he touched the hollow of his thigh; and the hollow of Jacob's thigh was out of joint, as he wrestled with him. And he said, Let me go, for the day breaketh. And he said, I will not let thee go, except thou bless me. And he said unto him, What is thy name? And he said, Jacob. And he said, Thy name shall be called no more Jacob, but Israel: for as a prince hast thou power with God and with men, and hast prevailed. And Jacob asked him, and said, Tell me, I pray thee, thy name. And he said, Wherefore is it that thou dost ask after my name? And he blessed him there. And Jacob called the name of the place Peniel: for*

Wrestling with God

I have seen God face to face, and my life is preserved. (Genesis 32:24-30)

This story has absolutely captured my attention for the last several months. It's funny because I used to get annoyed with this part of Jacob's story. I would often think, *Who did he think he was that he could wrestle with God?*

Then I entered my own wrestling match with God. What does it mean to wrestle with God? What does it feel like? It's hard to describe. The only way to describe it is that I have spent many hours on my knees begging God for His blessing. I've cried many, many tears asking God why He won't bless our ministry? Why He won't help things work out? I've questioned His goodness. I've asked hard questions. I've wrestled with trusting Him. I have written countless prayers and cries to God in my journal. I have asked, pleaded, argued, and questioned God so often. I feel that after several years of begging God and pleading with Him for His blessing and not feeling like I have gained it, I just want to wrestle with Him more. I feel like I can begin to understand why Jacob wrestled with the angel all night long and would not let him go until the angel blessed him.

Jacob did get his blessing, and I think there are a few lessons we can learn from his wrestling story.

Lessons from Jacob's Wrestling Match

First of all, we find that Jacob was alone when the wrestling match started. Often over the past few years, I have felt alone. Why is it that God allows us to feel such desperate loneliness? Then in the midst of our loneliness, He starts the wrestling process with us. We feel as though we have been marked and set aside for a time. I think God moves us into this isolated place to begin the wrestling process with us. Maybe He wants to see that we are not relying on anybody else or anything else. He takes every comfort away until we are left with only one option – to wrestle with God. He "pins us against the ropes" as they say. We have nowhere to go and no one to turn to. He pushes us into this place where we can only call out to God and plead with Him.

The second thing I see is that God came to Jacob during the night, not during the day. God started the wrestling match when it was still dark out. Jacob couldn't clearly see what he was doing. Are you in a night season right now? Are you waiting for daybreak? Are you waiting for God to break through on your behalf? Has He come to you in your darkest hour and let you begin to wrestle with Him – begin to ask hard questions, to plead with Him, to beg for His blessing? Jacob wrestled all night and would not let go until he received a blessing. He was so strong and persistent, in fact, that God touched Jacob's leg to give him a weakness. Do you actively engage God, or do you just let life happen? Jacob didn't. He wouldn't let God go until he received a blessing.

The third thing I see is the change that takes place in Jacob. Jacob did it; he wrestled all night with God and prevailed. He was able to let go of the garments of the One he wrestled with as a victor. How elated he must have been! Jacob had wrestled and not given up. In the end, he was victorious. God answered him and blessed him. But at what cost? Jacob would never be the same. He was forever physically changed. He forever walked with a limp. Everyone who encountered Jacob would see his limp. Maybe they would ask about it, maybe not. Can you imagine the stories he told? I have a feeling he probably told everyone he met. I'm sure that every time the weather changed, any time he walked for a while, or any time one of his grandkids sat on his bad leg, the pain rushing through his leg reminded him of the night he wrestled with God.

The last thing I notice is that his name was changed. He changed so much in that wrestling match that God felt it necessary to change his name. Think about it – his wrestling match changed his identity! I wonder what happened when he went to his family and told them his name was no longer Jacob. I wonder if they thought he was crazy? Or could they see the light in his eyes? Did they know without being told there that their dad and husband had spent the night wrestling with God and had prevailed?

Our Own Wrestling Match

What an incredible story! But what's that got to do with us? Well, we all want God's blessing. We beg God for it and pray for it, but do we ever consider the cost of what we are asking for? Wrestling with God for

His favor and blessing is no small feat. You can do it, but once you do, you will never be the same.

Is that why so many of us stop growing and serving and even walk away from our ministries? We beg and pray for God's blessing, but once the wrestling starts getting a little physical or difficult, we instantly ease up, call for a time-out, accuse Him of being unfair, and question His ability. We want to wrestle with God and receive His blessing in our lives and the lives of our family, but come on – we don't want to be hurt in the process! We don't want to get sweaty. We don't want any of the pain that is associated with it. We don't really want it *that* badly. Most of us, myself included, cry foul the second it gets a little heated.

What if we stayed in the battle? What if we stayed in the trenches and begged God, even demanded that He bless us? What would happen? I can tell you. The pressure turns on, life starts falling apart all around us, we start crumbling, our faith starts wavering, and we question the sanity of even doing this in the first place. Only those who stay in the battle are the ones who are truly changed, though. They are the ones who walk with a limp now, but the peace of God shines through their eyes.

Do you know anyone like this? Have you met someone who has wrestled with God and won? Such a person is rare because that kind of wrestling takes great faith – faith that God is Who He said He is and the outcome of the wrestling is going to be worth the pain you have to go through to get it.

We Have to Stick It Out

Oftentimes, we don't get to the blessing because we didn't stick it out in the wrestling stage. God begins to take us through something that we can only get through with His help, but all too quickly, our faith begins to evaporate. We begin to question God's goodness. We know that God is good, but is He going to be good to me? To be able to wrestle with God, we have to first be vulnerable and open ourselves up to Him. We have to trust that whatever He brings into our lives is worth the pain.

On the other hand, we can choose not to engage at all. We don't have to have God's favor and blessing in our lives. In fact, most people don't. Most people are content with where they are. Why risk it? Why bother messing with the life we have so carefully constructed around us? C. S. Lewis once said, "To love at all is to be vulnerable. Love anything and your heart will be wrung and possibly broken. If you want to make sure of keeping it intact, you must give it to no one, not even an animal. Wrap it carefully round with hobbies and little luxuries; avoid all entanglements. Lock it up safe in the casket or coffin of your selfishness. But in that casket, safe, dark, motionless, airless, it will change. It will not be broken; it will become unbreakable, impenetrable, irredeemable. To love is to be vulnerable."[8]

Was it Worth It?

I wonder what Jacob would say if we could ask him. I plan on doing that when I get to heaven. I wonder what his answer will be. I want to ask, "Was wrestling with God worth the pain, Jacob? You were forever affected and physically altered because of your encounter with God. Was it worth it?" I don't know what his answer will be, but I have a hunch he will say, "It was totally worth it! I was changed physically, yes, but not just in the way that I walk. I was changed physically in that my name is no longer Jacob, meaning 'supplanter'. Now my name is Israel, meaning 'he who prevails with God.' I was never ever the same, and I never wanted to go back to being Jacob. I was Israel, 'prince of God,' the man who prevailed with God. When you prevail with God, God prevails with you and in your life."

I imagine he would go on to tell us how blessed his life was and how different his life was from that point on. His only regret would probably be that he hadn't wrestled with God sooner.

Are you in the midst of wrestling with God right now? Are you begging Him to bless your kids and to pour out His blessings and favor in your life? Have you already begun to feel the pain of having an encounter with God – one that will forever change you? I have. I am even now in that process. I am holding onto God and pleading with Him to bless our ministry, our children, my husband, me, our finances, our friends, and our family. I don't want to live a mediocre, comfortable life—one that never sees the other side of a life so blessed by God because of having gone through the wrestling process.

Where are you? Are you in the same place? Can we encourage each other to hold on and keep wrestling? Jacob wrestled during the night until the morning light broke through. My morning hasn't broken through yet. It's still dark. I can't see, but I can feel Jesus' arms around me, and I am grabbing onto those arms and not letting go until He blesses me.

Starting Your Wrestling Match

Have you not yet begun your wrestling match with God? Are you content with sitting on the sidelines of life and ministry? Are you too comfortable with where you are? I encourage you to start your match. Beg for God's favor in your life and in the lives of your family. Don't just sit back, content to let life pass you by. You were meant for so much more than that! God has an incredible life of blessing for you, but it's on the other side of the wrestling match. Maybe it's a new ministry or a non-profit He wants you to start. Maybe He wants you to expand your family through adoption. Maybe He wants you to start a new business. Maybe He wants you to write a book. I don't know what it is, but I know it's on the other side of this wrestling match.

the Hidden Pain

I believe we all come to a time in our lives when we know God has something for us – something great. We feel like there is something more that God has for us, but we just can't see it yet. It seems so close yet feels so far away. I believe we can't see it because it only comes after wrestling with God.

So, I'm calling you out. Step out and engage God. Tell Him you are ready to move forward with what He has for you. Tell Him you know it's going to be difficult. It's going to be downright painful sometimes, but you are committing to staying in it until God shows you what it is you were created to do.

Just remember when you set out on this journey that you are not enough to make it on your own. You will need help. Remember Who it is you are wrestling with. Call out to Jesus when it's the darkest hours of the night, and you don't feel like you can keep going. Lean on Him when you need to rest. Ask Him for encouragement to keep going when you want to give up, but don't give up on wrestling with God. Keep praying, keep reading your Bible, and keep asking Him to show you something for the day. Keep loving other people. Keep showing up at church on Sunday, ready to worship and hear from God. Keep serving. Keep showing up and sharing with your small group. Keep asking God for His blessing on your life. Find out what He wants you to do with your life. Ask – no, *demand* that God blesses your life. Jacob did. He wouldn't let go until God did just that.

I'm not telling you to do something I haven't done. I have spent the last several years of my life wrestling with God. It's been painful and ugly at times. It's been the hardest thing I have ever gone through in my life, and I'm not done yet. But let me tell you some of the outflowing of my wrestling with God … I now blog at faithfullystepping.com, and I am writing this book to help others deal with their own hidden pain. I wouldn't be doing either of those things if I hadn't wrestled with God.

I now have such a deep peace in my heart that I am doing exactly what I was created to do. Even if no one reads this book or my blog, I am fulfilled. I enjoy writing. I enjoy blogging. I enjoy encouraging other women and inspiring them to be who God created them to be!

Chapter Thirteen

In the Midst of the Hidden Pain

I would love to tell you that God has turned everything around – that we now have hundreds coming to church and are experiencing incredible growth. I can't tell you that, because that is not the case. Instead, next Sunday morning, Matt will get up and preach to a group of less than fifty people. In fact, when Matt got up to start the service just a few Sundays ago, there were two people sitting in the audience. Yes, two! I can't begin to tell you how discouraging a practically empty room is! I understand that's how it is when you start, but we have been at this for eight years.

Which brings me to the question of this book …

the Hidden Pain

what do you do when you have been hurt so deeply by God? When you feel He is actively withholding His blessing? When the pain is so deep but not necessarily obvious to others?

I want to take a timeout for just a moment and say that through all of this, Matt and I have always praised God that our pain has not been what others have gone through. This is our trial, and while it is painful, we have always been so grateful that our trial has not been losing a child or a spouse or something equally painful.

Maybe you too have been hurt by God. Maybe like us, you know God could bless you with something you so deeply need and want, but He is not. Maybe it is something obvious that everyone knows and can pray for you, or maybe it is a hidden pain that very few know about. Maybe, my dear friend, you have been unable to get pregnant and become a mom, and every month is a reminder of how God hasn't answered your prayer. Maybe you have a bad relationship with a parent who hurt you deeply. Maybe your financial struggle is great and weighs on you daily; you're so tired of never having enough money to make ends meet. Maybe you were abused as a child, and you deal with the pain of that every day, and no one knows. Perhaps the spouse who promised to stay with you for better or for worse didn't keep their promise. They walked away, and now you are left to pick up the pieces of your broken heart and somehow move forward. Maybe you heard the words no one ever wants to hear, "You have cancer." Now you face the most difficult battle of your life. Perhaps you lost someone dear to you, and you feel your heart will never recover from breaking in two. Maybe you are tired of feeling lonely. You've watched all your friends get married and start a family, and that's all you've ever wanted. Why is God withholding it from you?

What do you do when God has hurt you so deeply? What do you do when you feel like maybe the life you are living is one that God is no longer blessing?

Behind the Scenes

As I sit here writing this, we just celebrated a big day at our church. Years of loving and serving people ... years of choosing to keep moving forward and not give up. On Sunday, we celebrated with moon bounc-

the Hidden Pain

es, cotton candy, hot dogs, face painting, and all kinds of fun. We loved on people, ate yummy food, and celebrated. We had a little over sixty people celebrate with us for the day, and we posted pictures on Facebook and Instagram. It was a great day!

Now let me tell you what it looks like behind the scenes, behind the pictures and smiling faces. At home, we don't have enough money to go grocery shopping for groceries for the week, so we don't. Malachi reminds me that I haven't gone grocery shopping, and I tell him we can't because we don't enough money. We pray as a family and ask God to provide for us. We check the mail for the day and find two more bills that need to be paid. We prepare to take the kids to a new dentist because we can no longer afford the one we have gone to for years. We work hard all week and prepare for another Sunday. It may be that only a handful of people come. Whether sixty people come or ten, we must prepare our best either way. So, Matt works on his sermon for Sunday, we work hard during the week on writing and blogging and other projects, and I homeschool the kids all week.

On Sunday morning, we will show up with smiles

on our faces and energy for the day. We will give of ourselves and serve and love on people. Once again, I will have to choose not to focus on what I am feeling. If I do, those feelings will leave me incapacitated to serve for the day.

I don't tell you all this so you will feel sorry for us. I just want to show you that I don't have the answers. I'm still working through it myself, but I do know I am not the same person I was eight years ago. God began a process of breaking me and remaking me that has taken me to the very edge of my faith in Him. I have been so close to walking away from it all, yet God has kept me from doing that. While I may not be finished with this season in my life, I know the ways God has chipped away at me. He has taught me so many things over these last eight years, and I don't want to waste my pain by not sharing them with somebody else. So in the remaining chapters of this book, I would like to share what God has taught me with you.

I believe that every person comes to a time in their life when they feel like God is no longer blessing them. For some, it may be a short time. Others may face something that they will deal with for the rest of their lives. When that time comes, my prayer is that the words and encouragement found in these next chapters will be hope and encouragement for your soul.

Chapter Fourteen

Learning Longsuffering

One night as our family was driving back into town, we turned off the highway and waited to turn onto a busy road. The driver in the car in front of us sat still without moving. After a few moments, somebody behind us honked, but the driver still didn't move. At this point, Matt was tired of waiting and drove around them. Well apparently, they did not appreciate that! They laid on their horn, sped up to pass us, and then jumped back in front of us. When we reached a red light and stopped behind them, the driver opened up her door, leaned out, and yelled at us. I have no idea what she said because we had a movie turned on for the kids. But I'm glad I couldn't hear her because I'm sure she had some choice words for us. We just laughed it off, but it reminded me that people are so impatient and think the world revolves around them. People can't put up with anybody doing anything even remotely offensive to them.

As a culture, we have lost the ability and vision for longsuffering. The dictionary defines longsuffering as "bearing injuries or provocation for a long time; patient." We don't bear injuries or provocations at all, let alone for a long period of time. The American mindset is, "Stand up for yourself. Don't let people walk all over you. Watch out for number one. You gotta take care of you because no one else is going to." With all of these kinds of thoughts running rampant, no wonder we don't have a clue about what it means to be longsuffering.

We walk away from our jobs the second we don't feel appreciated, we drop relationships as soon as they don't meet our needs, we move as soon as we get bored, and we are ready for a fight at a moment's notice. We don't allow anybody to take advantage of us or to walk all over us.

One of the lessons God has driven home to Matt and I these last eight years is longsuffering. He is teaching us what it means to stick with something and stay patient, even when the payoff isn't instant. Just because everything doesn't work out the way we think it should doesn't mean it's time to throw in the towel and move on.

Jesus' Example

Jesus is our example of longsuffering. Exodus 34:6 says, "And the Lord passed by before him, and proclaimed, The Lord, The Lord God, merciful and gracious, longsuffering, and abundant in goodness and truth."

God is so longsuffering towards us. He forgives us time and time again when we sin. He doesn't put a number on it; He just says if we keep asking, He will keep forgiving. "If we confess our sins, he is faithful and just to forgive us our sins, and to cleanse us from all unrighteousness." I John 1:9

We don't have an ounce of longsuffering. We ask God to bless us. We tell him we will do what He wants us to do with our lives, yet the second it doesn't all work out or something goes wrong, we backpedal. We second-guess ourselves. We talk ourselves out of doing whatever it is He wants us to do. We whine and complain about life being hard. We get frustrated, hurt, and even mad at God. If we pray and God doesn't answer right away, we get discouraged and give up. In his book, *The Circle Maker,* Mark Batterson says, "The reason many of us give up too soon is that we feel like we have failed if God doesn't answer our prayer. That isn't failure. The only way you can fail is if you stop praying...Sometimes the power of prayer is the power to carry on."[9]

We need to reach a point where we mature a little in our faith and in our relationship with God. When our kids are little, they love us and think the world of us, even after they've just been in trouble for something. As those same kids grow up, they reach a point where they must learn to trust our love. Maybe they don't understand why we wouldn't let them do what they wanted to do or go where they wanted to go, but we have a reason. We see the bigger picture. They don't. They must trust us and know that we have their best interest in mind.

It's the same in our relationship with God. We have to realize that He can see the entire picture. We can't. We make decisions based on the temporal, while He makes decisions based on the eternal. God says in Isaiah 55:8,9 "For my thoughts are not your thoughts, neither are your ways my ways, saith the Lord. For as the heavens are higher than the earth, so are my ways higher than your ways, and my thoughts than your thoughts."

We can't possibly know why God is doing what He is doing, so we can either choose to question Him all the time for infinite answers to our finite questions, or we can simply trust that He knows best.

Learning in My Current Stage

One Sunday at church, my husband said in a sermon, "I can only learn what I'm supposed to learn in the stage I'm in right now; I won't be able to learn it later." In that same message, he also said, "The only way for God to catch our attention is to come to us in our darkness."

C.S. Lewis is quoted as saying, "God whispers to us in our pleasures, speaks in our conscience, but shouts in our pain." If God wants to get your attention, He will do it. He will probably use pain to get your attention. Oh, it may not be physical pain. It might be a relationship that has ended, financial pressures, a child who has walked away from God, a job with no future in sight, a miscarriage, etc. I don't know what God has used in your life, but I know He will use something to draw you closer to Him than you ever were before.

We can choose to use our pain to help others, or we can just stay in our pain and let it be the unraveling of us. God loves us too much to let us stay the same. God can use our pain in miraculous ways.

Fanny Crosby's Story

Fanny Crosby is an example of someone who used her pain to help others. Fanny grew up blind. She could have been miserable. She had every right to not accomplish anything with her life, but she didn't use her pain as an excuse. Instead, she wrote beautiful poetry and music. Without her ministry, we wouldn't have some of the rich, beautiful hymns we have today such as "Blessed Assurance," "To God be the Glory," "Jesus, Keep Me Near the Cross," "Redeemed," "He Hideth

Learning Longsuffering

My Soul," "All the Way My Savior Leads Me," "Near the Cross," "Praise Him, Praise Him," and more.

A preacher once said to Fanny Crosby, "I think it is a great pity that the Master did not give you sight when he showered so many other gifts upon you." Since she had heard such comments before, Fanny Crosby responded quickly. "Do you know that if at birth I had been able to make one petition, it would have been that I was born blind?" said the poet who was only able to see for the first six weeks of her life. "Because when I get to heaven," she continued, "the first face that shall ever gladden my sight will be that of my Savior." What faith! What longsuffering she had![10]

What about a story of longsuffering from our day and age? Consider Nick Vujicic? Nick was born without arms or legs. He could have been bitter and angry at God, but instead, Nick travels around the world, sharing his story and the message of Jesus Christ.

When I think of Jesus' example of longsuffering and these other examples, it gives me the encouragement and motivation I need to keep going and stay faithful. When you are in the midst of life's painful moments and you feel like God is not blessing you, remember the longsuffering of our Savior and others. They didn't give up and walk away. They stayed faithful and are continuing to stay faithful.

My flesh tells me that we are stupid for hanging in there. If God really cared, He would have blessed by now; if we were really cut out for being church planters, it wouldn't be this difficult. The devil and the world shouts at us that we aren't good enough, successful enough, beautiful enough, talented enough, and on and on the list goes. The truth is, we're not, and on bad days, that's enough to make us want to start packing our bags and running away from the calling God gave us. We need to recognize the voice that is telling us these lies, and it's not God's voice!

God says we are loved, redeemed, the sons of God, more than conquerors, holy, heirs, friends, chosen, valuable, forgiven, precious, and much more. So on the Sundays we come home discouraged and defeated when there were only a few people in their seats on Sunday morning and when the bank account is low, I must remember to ignore the voice that tells me I am not enough because Jesus makes up for my "not enough." It's His power working through me. I am only responsible to do what He called me to do. The rest is up to Him.

What has you feeling like you are being tried with longsuffering? What has God asked you to bear over and over and over again? It's so tempting to just throw off the burden and walk away from it. Why deal with it? It would be so easy to just walk away from what God is calling you to do. But just as Jesus was faithful to fulfill the task God had for Him, we have to stay faithful to the tasks God has called us to.

Chapter Fifteen

Seeing God as My Father

One of the greatest stumbling blocks for me these past several years has been changing my view of God. I have realized over the years how much of my relationship with God has been a transactional one. If I do _____, then God will do _____. I have come to realize that our relationship with God doesn't work that way. He wants a relationship with us, and healthy relationships don't work that way.

God wants to deepen the relationship I have with Him. The problem is that to deepen our relationship, He has to take me further and further, deeper and deeper in my faith. That's really difficult to do. To go deeper in faith means you can't see God. He seems further and further away, and His goodness and favor seem more and more intangible. When this happens, it is so easy to just stop – stop going deeper, stop going forward, stop letting my heart get hurt. I think that is where a lot of us stop. We decide this relationship with God isn't worth the hurt and the hassle.

I have come so close from just walking away from it all – the church, being a pastor's wife, even my faith in God. Why haven't I? Honestly, it's because of God's mercy. He keeps pulling me back from the edge, getting me through one more day. One of the things that I continually turn to when I am struggling with my faith and my view of God is a phrase that Matt said to me one day in the car. This one phrase I believe has kept me from walking away from it all so many times, "What kind of a dad do you think you have?"

My husband Matt is such a good dad to our kids. He loves each of them so much! One of his favorite things to do is to take them on dates and buy them a toy. As much as I try to keep us on budget and not spoil the kids too much, there is Daddy, always ready to shower them with more love, grace, and gifts.

I see this all the time with my kids' dad, so why is it so hard for me to see my heavenly Dad this way? So many times I don't see God anything like this. I don't see God as my doting Father who wants to love on me, spend time with me, and shower me with gifts. Instead, I see Him more as a disapproving Dad, a Dad that focuses on all of my sins, failures, and shortcomings. I see the disciplinarian Dad, taking me through yet another trial to make me better, change me, grow me, and rub the rough edges off.

But God is so much more than just a strict disciplinarian Father. He is better at being a Dad than any earthly dad could ever be! How do I know this? His Word says so. Matthew 7:11 says, "If ye then, being evil, know how to give good gifts unto your children, how much more shall your Father which is in heaven give good things to them that ask him?" James 1:17 says, "Every good gift and every perfect gift is from above, and cometh down from the Father of lights, with whom is no variableness, neither shadow of turning."

Sometimes I wonder if God looks down at me when I'm feeling so discouraged and unworthy of His

the Hidden Pain

love and asks me, "What kind of Dad do you think you have?"

Just as Matt can see and understand what our kids need more than they can, so my Heavenly Father knows what I need more than I do. He knows the thing I have been so afraid to do is going to radically change me. He knows the thing I have been praying about for several years is not going to be answered the way I think it is, but His answer and plan is going to be so much better. His plan for me involves waiting right now because the rest of the story hasn't played out yet. If He brought it to pass now, I would only see half of the blessing He has prepared.

Friend, I don't know where you are in life right now. Maybe you are waiting for a relationship, and it just won't come. Maybe you are in financial need, and no matter how much you pray and work, you just can't get ahead. Perhaps it's a health problem, a relationship difficulty, or a job need that seems so out of reach. Maybe it's loneliness or failure. Maybe you have convinced yourself for so long (like I have) that you just don't deserve God's help and love and you are unworthy and unlovable.

I just want to remind you that our Heavenly Father is looking down on you and asking, "What kind of Dad do you think you have? I see the full picture, and it is more beautiful than you could ever imagine! Trust Me. Believe in Me. Find your joy in Me because I am your Father, and I love you more than you will ever understand this side of Heaven." Sometimes I just need to be reminded of a few of my favorite verses.

> *The Lord hath appeared of old unto me, saying, Yea, I have loved thee with an everlasting love: therefore with lovingkindness have I drawn thee. (Jeremiah 31:3)*

> *Call unto me, and I will answer thee, and show thee great and mighty things, which thou knowest not. (Jeremiah 33:3)*

> *As for God, his way is perfect: the word of the Lord is tried: he is a buckler to all those that trust in him. (Psalm 18:30)*

Existing, Not Living

A few months ago, I was reading *Breaking Busy: How to Find Peace and Purpose in a World of Crazy* by Alli Worthington. She was telling her story, and as I read what she wrote, it was if I had written those words. I felt them so strongly in my spirit that they could have been my words. Alli wrote, "I was miserable because I didn't trust him [God]. My worries were born out of my need to be in control, my desire to know what was next in my life, and a lack of gratitude for the grace head already given me."[11]

That was exactly what I felt. I was making myself miserable because I was striving so hard to do the right thing. I was so fearful of messing up and missing what God had for me.

Alli continued her thoughts, "I had been telling myself subconsciously that I couldn't be happy until I had answers straight from God. I was in a thought loop that set me up for misery. No wonder that even when life was going great, I had my head on the table begging God for more."[12]

Reading those words, I felt sucker-punched. That was me! No matter what prayers God was answering and no matter what He was doing, I wanted more. I felt like I didn't have an answer straight from God and therefore couldn't be content. Those words broke me. I was so full of stupid pride that even in my brokenness, I couldn't be broken.

Alli wrote, "By recognizing and releasing our fears to God, by letting go of our white-knuckled hold on the details of our lives, and by walking in the belief that He loves us and will provide for us, we find peace and comfort...and then he whispered to my spirit, 'Get up and live like you believe that I am going to take care of you'."[13]

I stopped reading, my eyes swimming with tears. This is what I so desperately needed to hear! I was existing; I wasn't living. I was wrapped up in fear and self-pity. When I read these words, it was as though the dam broke. I could no longer hold back the tears of grief, angst, and fear. They all came out.

This is what God is saying to us, "Go live like I am going to take care of you!" We teach our children that if God takes care of the birds, He will take care of us. We tell our kids that God knows how many hairs are on their heads. Yet as adults, we walk around in fear, not trusting that God, who has been faithful in the past, will be faithful again.

I am reminded of one of my favorite Bible verses, Lamentations 3:22-23. "It is of the Lord's mercies that we are not consumed, because his compassions fail not. They are new every morning: great is thy faithfulness." Praise God that His mercy and compassion never run out! Each day represents a fresh supply of compassion and mercy.

Webster's 1828 dictionary defines compassion as "a suffering with another; pity; commiseration; a mixed passion compounded of love and sorrow." If we put this definition back into the verse, it says that God suffers through our day with us in pity and commiseration mixed with love. Why does God do this? Because He knows and understands that we live in a sinful world full of grief, heartache, problems, and pain. He simply chooses to walk with us through the pain each and every day.

So if you feel like you can't make it through today, remember that Jesus is hurting with you. He is your Father and loves you so much. Lean on Him, and let Him carry you through today. Tomorrow will come, and just as sure as the sun will rise, Jesus will be there again to walk beside you once again.

Chapter Sixteen

Seven Don'ts God has Taught Me

As I think back on these past eight years, there are seven thoughts that God brings to mind. These are seven "don'ts" that God has really driven home over these years.

1. Don't diminish or underestimate your own pain.
One of the lies Satan led me to believe for so long and really caused some damage is that my pain is not as great as somebody else's pain. This has been so difficult for me and one of the reasons I almost didn't write this book. So, here it is – my life is not as hard as someone going through cancer, a parent losing a

child, a wife going through a divorce, and so on. Really, my pain is nothing compared to any of those things. During the past few years, I have stood by and watched the pain of those I love dearly as they have gone through some of the darkest trials of life. My trial is nothing compared to what some of them have gone through. However, I have to remember that this is my trial, and it is painful nonetheless.

I think one of the tricks Satan uses is to convince us that our problem is not as bad as someone else's. We feel guilty even mentioning anything about our problems to someone else, so we don't. That is a huge mistake. Stuffing down emotions only leads to depression. Once we get depressed, we are totally out of commission for Jesus to be able to use us in any way, and Satan wins. We must remember that our pain is just as important to God as anybody else's pain.

Psalm 34:18 says, "The Lord is nigh unto them that are of a broken heart; and saveth such as be of a contrite spirit." We must learn to give our pain to God and let Him deal with it. Don't keep it to yourself. If we're not careful, we will begin to be resentful toward God. Mark Batterson says, "The hardest thing about praying hard is enduring unanswered prayers. If you don't guard your heart, unresolved anger toward God can undermine faith. It's easy to give up on dreams, give up on miracles, give up on promises. We lose heart, lose patience, lose faith. And like a slow leak, it often happens without us even knowing it until our prayer life gets a flat."[14]

2. *Don't diminish other people's pain.*
Secondly, after we learn to not devalue our own pain, we must learn not to devalue other people's pain. This can be really difficult. Sometimes we just can't take other people and their problems, especially when we are going through something ourselves. I get it; I am guilty of this so often. My world can come crashing down during the week; and on Sunday, I go to church to try to minister to other people. Their problems may seem like nothing compared to what I am facing. We have to remember that even if it isn't a big deal to *me*, that doesn't mean it isn't a big deal to *them*!

I also need to remember that God has not promised grace to me for someone else's problem. He promises grace for me to carry *my* burdens. I remember talking to a lady at church one Sunday morning about the horrible week I just had. She asked me how my week was, so I took that as a green light to open up and tell her about it. I told her how bad my week was, what I was struggling with, and the desperation I felt. I kid you not, she didn't bat an eye before she started talking about everything she was going through in her own life.

It's hard, but that's kind of how life works. Everybody is going through their own problems and difficulties. Most of the time, other people don't have time to deal with you and your problems. If I'm not careful, this can (and has at times) make me bitter toward other people. In *Life-Giving Leadership,* Julia Mateer says, "The greatest tactic of the enemy is to get you to stop loving and ministering to others and to retreat to where it is safe... out of commission and out of life. If we let issues and disappointments sit and fester in our souls, they will be harder to deal with later. Emotional anger not dealt with will lead to sinful bitterness. Remember, no matter our circumstances, the state of our hearts will determine the direction or our lives and our leadership." [15]

We have to be so careful not to let bitterness in, or it will destroy us. Hebrews 12:15 says, "Looking diligently lest any man fail of the grace of God; lest any root of bitterness springing up trouble you, and thereby many be defiled."

In her book, *Church of the Small Things,* Melanie Shankle writes, "God has a script written for each and every one of us, no matter who we are or what we've done or how ill-equipped for the adventure we feel. We are all climbing our own versions of Mount Everest and have no idea if our oxygen will last or if an avalanche will come, but God does. We can never underestimate the grace and the strength he will give us for whatever he is calling us to do and whatever challenges we'll face. What he has planned for us is higher and deeper than anything we could ever hope to achieve on our own."[16] Just as that is true for us, it is true for others.

3. Don't put on God something He didn't promise.

This lesson continues to still be really hard for me to learn. I need to be so careful that I am not holding God to something He never said He would do. God never told us we would have a big church. God never told us everything would work out perfectly, and we wouldn't have problems starting the church. He didn't even promise us that we would be successful. He only asked us to follow His leading and start a church. Our job is simply to obey and stay faithful. My definition of success is different from God's definition. My timetable is different from God's timetable. If I'm not careful, I will start to wallow in my problems until I become filled with self-pity. Once that happens, I'm pretty much useless to God and His work and to my family.

4. Don't compare.

Comparison is so easy to do! All I have to say here is social media, right? We think we are doing a good job in what God has called us to do until we see how somebody else is doing his or her ministry. I think we do so much damage in comparing ourselves to others on social media. We all know that we only put our best days on display. We know it in our heads, but unfortunately, we don't let that stop affecting our hearts. II Corinthians 10:12 says, "For we dare not make ourselves of the number, or compare ourselves with some that commend themselves: but they measuring themselves by themselves, and comparing themselves, **are not wise.**" I don't think God could put it any clearer than that. When we compare ourselves to others, we are not wise. So why do we do it? Because it is in our very nature to do so. Do you have to teach kids how to compete with each other? Nope. It comes naturally at a very young age. We all want to be the best – to be someone special.

We need to remember that God made us just the way we are. In Jeremiah 1:5, God says to Jeremiah, "Before I formed thee in the belly I knew thee; and before thou camest forth out of the womb I sanctified thee, and I ordained thee a prophet unto the nations." Psalm 139:13,14 says, "For thou hast possessed my reins [kidneys]: thou has covered me in my mother's womb. I will praise thee; for I am fearfully and wonderfully made; marvelous are thy works; and that my soul knoweth right well." God has made each of us uniquely different for the exact purpose and plan He has for our lives. The best way to accomplish God's plan for my life is to worry about what I am supposed

the Hidden Pain

to be doing, not about what anybody else is supposed to be doing.

A perfect example of this is seen in the life of Peter. One day, the disciples are enjoying a meal with Jesus after His resurrection. It is the last meal they will ever have with Him. Peter has just come back to Jesus after denying Him at His trial and crucifixion. Peter was preparing to eat and saw John hanging out very close to Jesus. John is referenced in the Bible as "the disciple whom Jesus loved." Peter knew that, and his jealousy kicked in when he saw John so close to Jesus. Peter turned to Jesus and asked, "Jesus, what will *this* man do?" Jesus answered him with the best answer. I love it! Jesus said, "What is that to thee? Follow thou me." Jesus could have blasted Peter. After all, just days before, Peter had denied and cursed when telling others that he didn't know Jesus. Instead, Jesus graciously reminded Peter that he needed to worry about himself and not John. See, we are not alone! Even Jesus' disciples struggled with comparison.

The best way for us to accomplish God's purpose for our lives is to keep our eyes forward. Don't look around at what everybody else is doing.

Remember that there is no shame in being who God created you to be. You have nothing to prove to anybody else. In fact, if you struggle with this like I do, I would suggest you read two specific books – *Nothing to Prove: Why We Can Stop Trying So Hard* by Jennie Allen and *Unmasked: Uncovering the Shame that Says You're Not Enough* by my husband, Matt Manney. Both are available on Amazon.

5. Don't Condemn yourself.
One of the biggest mistakes I make again and again is condemning myself. I listen to the voice in my head that says I am not doing enough, I am not enough, and I will never be enough. First of all, that is all true. That's why God sent Jesus to redeem us. Jesus is Enough. As my husband, Matt, often says which I need to remember, "It's not about you, it's not because of you, and it's not up to you." That can really take the wind out of your sails, but it's so true. Everything is not about me. It's not always about just trying harder, even though that's usually what the voice in my head whispers to me. What I am going through is what God has chosen to use to draw me closer to Him and to

make me more like Him.

One of my favorite verses is I Peter 5:10: "But the God of all grace, who hath called us unto his eternal glory by Christ Jesus, after that ye have suffered a while, make you perfect, **stablish, strengthen, settle** you." God has specifically planned the events in my life to establish, strengthen, and settle me. I don't know about you, but I need settling. I get so wrapped up in worries, fears, pressures, and failures, that I need God to settle me. The idea of God settling me makes me think of being wrapped up in a big, soft blanket and letting His peace wash over me.

There is a story in the Gospels about a woman caught in the act of adultery. The men of the city caught her and threw her at the feet of Jesus. They told Jesus what they caught her doing and then sat back to watch what He was going to do. I can't even begin to imagine this woman's humiliation. Can you? What a horrible situation to be in! Jesus doesn't say anything. He simply writes with a stick in the sand. I have no idea what He wrote because the Bible doesn't tell us. Whatever it was, it was powerful because one by one, the men of the city stalked off.

Soon, only Jesus and the woman were left. We pick up the story in John 8:10,11: "When Jesus had lifted up himself, and saw none but the woman, he said unto her, Woman, where are those thine accusers? hath no man condemned thee? She said, No man, Lord."

I absolutely love Jesus' response, "And Jesus said unto her, Neither do I condemn thee: go, and sin no more." Jesus didn't condemn her, a woman caught in the very act of adultery; yet He didn't condone it either. He simply told her to stop sinning.

So why do we condemn ourselves? This isn't about trying harder; it's not about doing better or working longer hours. It's about Jesus coming through on our behalf and working in an incredible way so there is no way we could ever take credit for it!

6. Don't take it personally.

This one is tricky. Here's the deal – life is hard. This world is full of sin and sinful people. We can't let that blindside us. Life happens. Sometimes family moves away; sometimes good friends disagree and move out of your life; sometimes co-workers just don't like you. Some of it is just life, and we have to be careful that we don't turn everything into a spiritual case. Life happens, and sometimes you just can't fix it. When those things happen, we must try not to take it personally. Not everything is about us, and we can't fix everything. Sometimes the best thing we can do is not take things personally and let them go.

7. Don't quit.

No matter what, I can't quit, and neither can you. Our spouses are counting on us, our children are counting on us, our friends are counting on us, and those who we are going to invite to church in the future are counting on us. Why go through all the pain and frustration just to quit and throw in the towel now? This is the last of the list of "don'ts" God has taught me over the past eight years, and I think it is the most important. There have been so many times when the most intelligent thing to do would be to quit.

A little while back, a man from the church I grew up in told my husband, "You know, most people would have quit by now." Yeah, most people probably would have. It's only by God's grace that we haven't, but we haven't. We're still holding on to hope.

Seven Don'ts God has Taught Me

C.S. Lewis said, "To walk out of His will is to walk into nowhere."[17] That's exactly how we feel. If we walk away now from the church, where would we go? What would we do? I feel like we would be walking into nowhere. Lewis also stated, "God cannot give us a happiness and peace apart from Himself, because it is not there. There is no such thing."[18]

The big picture is that we will be happy and at peace when we are doing what God created us to do. For us now, that means to stay faithful in our church plant. We choose to focus on what we know we are supposed to do and leave the rest in God's capable hands. Jenni Allen said it best when she said, "Nothing can stand against the force of God moving through a soul completely in love with Him. It is the simple things that will change the world. You do the simple work of loving God and loving people. It is messy, hard, and not too glamorous. And that sounds like Jesus."[19]

Chapter Seventeen

Understanding the True Meaning of Success

"I just don't think pastoring is my thing," I looked up, startled at what I had just heard.

"What?" I asked.

Matt looked at me and repeated himself, "I just don't think pastoring is my thing." I immediately jumped in to tell him all of the reasons why his statement was untrue.

"That's just Satan trying to discourage you. You are a good pastor. People tell you all the time how much they enjoy your preaching. *I* enjoy your preaching and learn something every week," I said passionately.

He looked at me and then quietly said, "They might

like my preaching, but not enough to come back." All my rebuttals were drowned out by the look in his eyes. I knew some of what he was saying was true. I sat there quietly and pondered what he was saying. *Is there any truth to that? Are we failures? Should we just quit?*

I can't tell you how many times Matt and I have repeated this scene. Usually the conversation takes place on a Sunday after church or first thing Monday morning. Oh, the words aren't always exactly the same, but it's the same conversation over and over again.

After enough of these conversations, Matt and I knew that if we were going to stay in this for the long haul, we were going to have to redefine our definition of success. I had already defined what success looked like in my personal life, but now we needed to determine what it looked like in our ministry.

So, what is success? How do we know if we are successful? How do we know if God is pleased with us? How do we know we are doing what He created us to do? After years of reading books, studying the Bible, and having hundreds of conversations about it, we have redefined what success in our ministry looks like to us.

This is what we have come up with ... when it really comes down to it, success is not about achievement. *Success is simply obedience to God.* Success is not being the best. It's about following through with what God asked me to do. C.S Lewis is quoted as saying, "It is not your business to succeed, but to do right; when you have done so, the rest lies with God."[20]

Matt came up with a few questions to use to evaluate our success:

1. Did I do what God asked?
2. Am I doing what He created me to do?
3. Am I doing the best I can with the abilities I have, the resources available, and the opportunities I've been given?

God called Matt and I to start Greater Philly Church. We just need to focus on staying faithful. Whether that means preaching and caring for twenty people or five hundred people, the mission stays the same.

We don't get to plan out all the details of our lives. Everything that happens is not in our control. God is in control. More times than not though, as soon as something doesn't go according to plan, we begin questioning ourselves and God. We want to know how everything is going to work out, and we want to know it right now! Unfortunately, that is not how God works. Can you testify? I know I can!

Job's Example

Time and time again, God has used the story of Job in my life to drive this point home. The book of Job has many amazing hidden gems in it. If you have been around church for any length of time, you are probably familiar with the story of Job. Job's ten children died on the same day that he lost all of his livestock and servants. Soon after that, Job lost his health. Job went from being an incredibly wealthy and well-known man of means to a nobody who lost everything.

Job 23 finds Job in the midst of his suffering. He is desperately trying to understand what is going on in his life and where God is during this time. He cries out to God, "Oh that I knew where I might find him [God]! that I might come even to his seat! I would order my cause before him, and fill my mouth with arguments. I would know the words which he would answer me, and understand what he would say unto me." Job 23:3-5

As you read these words, can you feel Job's desperation? His greatest desire in the midst of his trial was to find God. He wanted to argue his case before God. He wanted to ask the questions that we all desire to ask of God when we are in a trial. Why God? Why me? What have I done wrong? Where are You? Do you see my pain? Do you care? Job wanted to ask God these questions; then he wanted to hear God's answers. What would God say? Job wanted to know and understand God's answers. The next few words out of Job's mouth give a really good picture of the wisdom Job has. Job said in the first part of verse 6, "Will he plead against me with his great power? No."

The word plead here means "to grapple, to contend, to debate." Job pondered, "If I was able to plead my case directly with God Himself and ask Him all my questions, would He debate with me?"

Don't miss Job's answer. He answers for God – "No". Deep in his heart, Job knew that even if he had a chance to talk to God about his pain and his hurt, God would not use His power to force Job to see things His way.

God doesn't give Job an explanation, and Job recognized that God didn't owe him one. Similarly, God doesn't owe us any explanations. Even if He did give us an explanation, our finite minds couldn't understand it. God is not going to fight or debate with us to prove His point. That is not how our loving Heavenly Father works. Notice the next few words from Job in chapter 23. "Will he plead against me with his great power? No; but he would put strength in me."

Job understood that God was not going to debate with him to answer his questions. Instead, Job understood that God would simply fill him with strength to endure his trials. As much as we want answers, I don't know that it would change anything. I don't even know if I would want to know. It could be painful. What if God told me the reason why our church plant won't take off right now? Would I want to know? If God were to tell my mom why she has dealt with a debilitating disease for most of her life, would it make it any easier? If God told my dear friend why her precious grandson passed away from cancer just weeks before his 20th birthday, would the pain be any easier to bear?

As much as we want answers (even demand them), God knows we probably couldn't handle them, so until we get to Heaven, God just gives us strength to handle what comes our way. My life verse is Psalm 18:30, "As for God, his way is perfect: the word of the Lord is tried: he is a buckler to all those that trust in him." Verse 32 goes on to say, "It is God that girdeth me with strength, and maketh my way perfect."

God has His reasons for doing things the way He does them. I may never understand why, but I trust Him. The next few verses in Job always haunt me when I read them. "Behold, I go forward, but he is not there; and backward, but I cannot perceive him. On the left hand, where he doth work, but I cannot behold him: he hideth himself on the right hand, that I cannot see him." Job 23:8-9

Have you ever felt like Job? That no matter which way you turn, you can't see God working in your life? Sometimes, life gets so complicated. We try our best to do all the "right" things. We go to church, read our Bibles, love and care for our families, and are kind to

the Hidden Pain

others. We do everything we are supposed to do, yet we don't feel His presence. We can't see Him working in our life, and we sense that His hand of blessing and favor is not on us. What do you do when you hit a dry spell like this?

Job experienced deep discouragement when he wrote those verses. During a time of tragedy, he looked for God but couldn't find Him anywhere. He knew God's hand of blessing had been taken off his life, but he doesn't know why or what to do to change it. Job questions God's presence during this difficult time, but he moves on rather quickly in the next verse. "But he knoweth the way that I take: when he hath tried me, I shall come forth as gold. Job 23:10

During this season of life when he couldn't see God, Job chose to believe that God was still actively involved in His life. He trusted that God was watching over him and taking notice of what Job was doing. It's during times of discouragement and uncertainty that I have to choose to believe that God is actively present and watching over me. I have to trust that He sees me, even though I may not be able to see Him right now.

Understanding the True Meaning of Success

Sometimes I wonder if the emptiness and uncertainty we feel is just God's way of reminding us that this world is not our home. He doesn't want us getting too comfortable here. In his book, *Imagine Heaven*, John Burke says, "Maybe the reason we never feel fully satisfied in this life is because we were created for the life to come."[21] We will never feel fully satisfied and feel God's complete favor until we finish our race here on earth and spend eternity with the One Who created us. Once we are at His side, we will be completely whole and feel His favor forever. Until then, my job is to simply do what God has asked me to do and stay faithful to Him. That's the simple definition of success.

Chapter Eighteen

Getting Back Up Again

Our eight-year-old daughter Madison participated in pony camp this past summer and learned an important lesson about getting back up again. She loves horses and had been begging to have horse-riding lessons. My friend Kelley told me she was going to host a pony camp and would love to have Madison be part of it for the week. We agreed to let Madison give it a try. Every day from 9-3, Madison went to pony camp. She learned how to ride, how to groom and care for the horse, and so much more.

On the last day, all of the parents showed up to watch the children perform. Our family sat and watched and clapped as the kids showed us what they had learned. We whistled and cheered when it was Madison's turn, and she had a huge smile on her face. It was going great until something spooked her horse. Everything happened at once. Kelley yelled at Madison to hang on and came running from the other side of the corral while Madison's helper dropped the reins of her horse and Madison fell off. A second after falling, my friend grabbed Madison in one arm and the reins of the horse in the other. We all let out the breath we had been holding.

It was absolutely silent as everybody watched Madison to see if she was okay. She kept her head buried in Kelley's neck. Matt walked over and took her from Kelley and brought her to me. By the time I got her, she was sobbing quietly. Madison is usually not very emotional, so it surprised me to see her so worked up. She clung to me as I carried her away from the corral and into the house. I tried to pull her away from me to look at her face, but she wouldn't let go. I just held her for the next twenty minutes or so.

After she finally calmed down, she told me the horse stepped on her foot when she fell. Matt came in and checked to make sure her foot was okay. After Madison settled down, Kelley came in to check on her. She knelt before Madison and talked to her for a little bit. She told Madison that before she left, she wanted her to get back on the horse. I inwardly thought, *Good luck with that*! I know my daughter, and when she sets her mind on something, there is no moving her.

When we went back outside to watch the rest of her friends perform, Madison was mostly quiet and just sat with Matt and me. She told me a few times she didn't want to get back on the horse, but I didn't say anything. Eventually, the show was over, and it was time to face the music. I pretty much dragged Madison to the entrance to the corral. She did not want to go in there, and I was pretty sure nobody was going to get her on that horse. I knew I wouldn't be able to force her. I just hoped Kelley could work her magic and somehow convince Madison to get back on the horse.

I'm not even sure how it really happened, but a few minutes later, a very reluctant Madison sat on her horse again, looking scared to death. I was nervous watching her. It took quite a bit of coaxing, but Madison finally started riding again. After a few minutes, she started smiling again. Everybody cheered for her as she went through each of the elements she missed after she fell.

When she finished, everybody cheered, and Madison climbed off her horse with a huge smile on her face. She was all smiles for the rest of the day, and on the way home, she talked about going to pony camp next year. I must have told her a hundred times how proud I was of her for facing her fears and getting back on the horse again.

When Life Knocks Us Down

Watching Madison reminded me so much of how life knocks us down sometimes. We get knocked on our backside by something we didn't see coming. We get stepped on and hurt, and our hopes and dreams come crashing down.

For me, the loss of income and major financial burdens combined with the disappointment of things not turning out better for our church were my "falling off the horse" moment. What makes those times worse is that when we are down, we get stepped on. For me,

Getting Back Up Again

I was stepped on by the criticism we received and the loss of friendships. It's the whole "getting kicked while you're down" experience. It isn't enough that we are hurt and in pain from getting knocked off our feet. Someone has to come along and criticize and hurt you, which only makes the situation worse. When that happens, we have a choice to make. We can let our circumstances and critical people keep us down, or we can choose to get back up again. Honestly, we have every right to stay down.

When everything fell apart for us, nobody expected us to keep going. People expected us to quit the church. If we had walked away, our friends would have been hurt, but nobody would have faulted us (except our critics). We would have had grounds to walk away. People would have understood. Our family would have understood. There was pain and heartbreak combined with disappointment and dreams that had died. We had to decide if we would stay down or get back up again and keep going.

After Madison's fall and getting stepped on, I had no intention of making her get back on the horse. If she wouldn't have tried again, I certainly wouldn't

the Hidden Pain

have faulted her – nobody would have. The fact that she got back on the horse again was an inspiration to all of us. When you and I don't stay down, it's an inspiration to others.

In those moments after loss, pain, and hurt, all we want to do is stay on the ground. When that happens, it's okay to stay down for a little bit. We may need to cry because of the fear, the pain, the loss of a dream, etc. It took time for me to recover from the blow we took. We didn't walk away from the church; we kept showing up every Sunday morning. I did, however, take a break from certain things. I couldn't face people. During this season of our lives, we didn't stop our growth group on Tuesday nights, but we did stop hospitality on Sunday afternoons.

Our growth group knew what we were going through and walked through it with us. Other than that, I couldn't have people over for a time. Even family was difficult to be around because talking always led back to what we were going through.

Matt deals with things by talking about the problem. I deal with problems by being quiet and keeping it close to my heart. He needed to talk through the difficulties with his family while I needed time by myself to heal. So on many Sunday afternoons, I would make lunch and eat with Matt's family; then I would disappear into my room. I would often take one of my little girls with me, and we would take a nap together on the bed. I know this frustrated Matt at times, but I needed space to heal. I knew it wouldn't be forever, and Matt was gracious to give me the time I needed for healing.

Eventually after several months, I got to a place where I could deal with people again. I started spending more time with Matt's family on Sunday afternoons. After a while, I got to a place where we could start having company again. After we got settled into our new home, we started having families from church over on Sunday afternoons again.

Three Things I Wish Someone Would Have Told Me

When our dreams come crashing down, when failure blindsides us, or when hurt and betrayal rocks the very core of who we are, it is so tempting to curl into a ball and not face life. Let me tell you what I wish

the Hidden Pain

someone had told me during this time in my life.

First of all, take time to heal. It's okay to cry; it's okay to feel broken-hearted. It's okay to take a break from ministering to people for a time. It won't be forever; it's just for a time.

Secondly, don't belittle what you are going through. Yes, other people have gone through much worse. There will always be someone who has it worse than you, but that's not your story. You are living your own life, dealing with your own problems. Let yourself grieve, cry, get angry, and fully experience your emotions.

Lastly, don't stay down. After a time, ask God to help you find the inner strength to stand back up, shake the dust off, face people again, and ultimately "climb back on the horse." If we're not careful, we will wrap ourselves in a protective bubble and won't try anything outside our comfort zone again. Don't let this experience dictate your future.

It's easy to climb on the horse the first time, but it's much harder after you've been tossed off. Starting a new job is easy, but it's hard to start a job after losing the last one. It's exciting to get married the first time, but it's scary to try it a second time after divorce. Putting yourself out there for others is good until you get criticized; then it's painful. It's thrilling to start a business, but it's terrifying to try again after the last one failed.

We must remember that fear can destroy us and keep us from moving forward again. We fear getting hurt again, failing again, and not being able to get back on our feet. We have to choose not to fear; fear is not of God. We are reminded of this in II Timothy 1:7, " For God hath not given us the spirit of fear; but of power, and of love, and of a sound mind."

I John 4:18 has says this to say regarding fear, "There is no fear in love; but perfect love casteth out fear: because fear hath torment. He that feareth is not made perfect in love."

I love how Eugene Peterson paraphrases that same verse. "There is no room in love for fear. Well-formed love banishes fear. Since fear is crippling, a fearful life—fear of death, fear of judgment—is one not yet fully formed in love." (MSG)

Fear will always keep us from moving forward. Fear is of the Devil, and his ultimate goal is to keep us from accomplishing anything for God. He uses fear to do that. Fear is crippling; but with God's help, we can push aside our fear and move forward.

Madison became a hero at pony camp. She didn't do any fancy tricks, and she didn't do anything more complicated than anybody else. She simply chose to get back up when she fell down. Sometimes being the hero is simply getting back up and trying again. I don't know what has knocked you down, but I am here to encourage you to get back up again. Don't stay down. Proverbs reminds us to keep getting back up, no matter how many times we have fallen or failed. "For a just man falleth seven times, and riseth up again." Proverbs 24:16

Stand up, brush off the dirt, and try again. Whatever it is God has called you to do, He will empower you to do it. Stick with it, and see it through. You will look back and see that getting back up again was the best decision you ever made.

Chapter Nineteen

Navigating the Storms

We all want miracles in our lives. We want to see God do for us what we have seen Him do for other people. We want him to do something amazing! The problem is that in order to have a miracle, you must have a problem so big that only a miracle can save you. And that's where most of us get stuck. It's really hard to be in a place where the only thing that can save you is a straight-up miracle from God. Usually, when we need a miracle from God, it's because we are in in the midst of a storm.

There is a story in the book of Matthew that tells us about a storm the disciples were in:

the Hidden Pain

> *And straightway Jesus constrained his disciples to get into a ship, and to go before him unto the other side, while he sent the multitudes away. And when he had sent the multitudes away, he went up into a mountain apart to pray: and when the evening was come, he was there alone. But the ship was now in the midst of the sea, tossed with waves: for the wind was contrary. And in the fourth watch of the night Jesus went unto them, walking on the sea. And when they were come into the ship, the wind ceased.* (Matthew 14:22-25,32)

The disciples were in a storm. The waves crashed against their ship. It was nighttime, and they were scared. In their darkest hour, Jesus went to them. In the ninth hour when all hope was lost, Jesus went to them. After Peter walked on the water, Jesus got into the boat with them, and the storm ceased. There are lessons we can learn about going through storms in our own lives by watching the disciples go through their storm.

First, the disciples went into a storm right on the heels of a spiritual high. Let me give you the setting for this storm. The disciples had spent the entire day listening to Jesus preach and then trying to come up with a plan to feed everyone. Jesus stepped in and bailed them out by taking a little boy's lunch and blessing it. The boy's lunch ended up feeding more than 5,000 people. The disciples came from that and headed right into a storm.

Don't let this little detail slip by. So many times, the storms in our lives come right after spiritual victories. If we're not careful, we don't see the storm coming and don't recognize it for what it is. Before we know it, we are smack dab in the middle of a storm, totally unprepared and desperate for help from God.

Second, if there had been no storm, they would have had no need for Jesus to go to them. I don't know about you, but I have a really hard time being thankful for the storms in my life. However, Jesus comes to us during the storms in our lives when we are the most fearful and scared. If there wasn't any storm, there wouldn't be any drawing close to Jesus out of fear and desperation. God knows our frailty. He knows we are not good about actively seeking Him until we get into trouble, so as a loving Father, God sends a storm so we can do nothing but draw closer to Him.

Third, the storm came upon the disciples during the fourth watch of the night. The fourth watch of the night would have been between 3 a.m. and 6 a.m. Think of how tired the disciples were at this point and how dark it would have been. They say it's usually the darkest before it starts to get light. The disciples were exhausted from their long day. It was the darkest hour of the night, and a storm came out of nowhere.

Fourth, don't underestimate the fact that Jesus went to them. This is so important. Jesus was God. He didn't need to go to the disciples to calm the storm. He could have calmed the storm from where He was on the shore, but He went to them. Why? Was it for His sake? No. It was for their sake. Don't miss this. Jesus comes to us in our storms. He did leave the disciples alone for a time during the storm, then He came to them.

Lastly, after Peter walked on the water with Jesus, Peter and Jesus climbed into the boat. Once Jesus was in the boat, the wind ceased. When storms come, Jesus enters the storm with us and goes through it with us. Then He calms it. I can't imagine the kind of peace the disciples must have felt as soon as Jesus stepped into their boat. It's like they could finally let out the breath they had been holding. They knew everything was going to be okay now. No matter what we are going through, we can have peace when we remember that God is with us in the midst of our storm, even when it may not feel like it or not look like it. This is when we can't let our emotions rule our hearts. We have to choose to trust that God is with us during this storm, and He will see us safely through it.

We all experience storms. My storm has lasted for several years. What about you? Has your storm lasted far longer than you ever thought possible? Maybe you just came through one, or maybe there is a storm coming that you can't foresee.

Remember when you are in the storm and it's the very darkest, Jesus will come to you and be with you during your storm and calm it. Jesus promised His presence will always be with us. Hebrews 13:5 says, "… for he hath said, I will never leave thee, nor forsake thee."

Chapter Twenty

When God Doesn't Provide

I think probably the most difficult thing I have dealt with over these last eight years is the feelings I had when God didn't provide. It's sounds so ungodly to be writing these words, but I want to get to the heart of what I mean.

When somebody goes through any type of financial hardship or trial, we automatically throw out, "God will provide." I believe this. I have always believed this. I have said it to other people hundreds of times because God had always provided in my life. Whenever I had a need in the past, I always prayed, and God always provided. It was His job. He says He will meet our needs. He says not to worry about tomorrow. My entire life, when I had a need, I would pray, and God always met that need. When I was young and we needed money for groceries, God provided. Somebody would show up at our home with groceries. When we needed money for work on our car, we would pray, and the money would come in. When I couldn't pay for my college bill, God provided. When Matt and I couldn't afford a medical bill, God provided. Every time we had a need, God always provided. Now it may not have been on my timetable, but God always came through.

Now fast forward to my family in major financial crisis, and God didn't provide. When we ran out of money in our savings and our bank account, we had to start paying all our bills with our credit card. We kept praying for God to provide, but He didn't. Soon, our credit card was maxed out. Neither Matt nor I had ever come even close to maxing out a credit card before. This was uncharted waters.

During this time, close friends and even family would say, "It's okay. God will provide." It would make me so angry. I wanted to shout back, "But He's not! God's not providing! He hasn't provided the last several months. That's why we had to put all our bills and food and gas on the credit card. Now our credit card is maxed out!"

I was so angry and frustrated, but beneath it all, I was desperately broken and confused. Why wasn't God providing? I had always had incredible faith. Prior to this mess, I never once doubted that God would meet my needs. No matter how bleak things looked, I was always the one touting, "God will provide." And He always had ... until now.

Many times, I begged and cried for God to help us. I can't tell you how many times I faced empty cupboards and an empty refrigerator, trying to make just one more meal for our family.

Developing a Deeper Faith

This past year and a half rocked my faith. It's only now that I can look back with just a little clarity, and I've realized something about my faith. My faith was weak. I thought it was strong, but it wasn't. I had what I call a one-to-one faith with God when it came to provision. When I had a need, I prayed; and God would answer. Prayer… answer. He didn't always answer right away, but He always came through. I understood about things such as illnesses and loss and other requests that God may never answer. But God providing for us? That was easy. My faith had always worked for me in the past. Now, I was in unchartered waters. This was entirely new. I had never dealt with God not providing. God was taking my faith deeper, and it was painful. This new faith required me to trust God, even when He didn't provide. This was a much deeper faith. Now it was affecting my kids.

God was saying, "Amanda, will you choose to trust me even when I don't pay your bills on time? Will you believe that I am good, even when it doesn't seem like it?" That's real faith! Easy faith is when you ask for help, and God provides. It takes deep faith when you ask God to provide, and He doesn't.

Obviously, because our family is still alive and breathing, God eventually provided for us. A friend paid our mortgage for us one month. Several times, friends and family brought us groceries. We would get a random check or cash from family or someone we knew. It was just enough to get us by. Eventually, Matt started picking up hours for Uber Eats and then Amazon. Then we moved, and the financial strain lessened a little.

We are still digging out of the financial hole we were in. There's not a nice bow to put on our problems to tie up all the loose ends and say, "It all worked out." We are still getting back on our feet. It's because of the generosity of amazing people God has used in our lives that we are still ministering in the Philadelphia area. Several times, we really thought that we would have to close the doors of our church and move on, but God has kept that from happening. God has helped us gain a little bit of traction, and I know He is going to keep providing for us so we can stay here.

With a little bit of clarity now, I can look back and see how God got us through. Even so, I do believe that God chose not to provide for us for a time. When I tell people this, they argue with me. People can say what they want. We are the ones who lived it, and I can honestly say that God did not always provide for us. I believe He allowed us to come to the absolute end of ourselves to show us what real faith is. Real faith is scary, let me tell you! Yet my faith is stronger today than it was a year ago. It seems so counterintuitive that God would not provide for us so that our faith could grow, but somehow, in God's amazing wisdom, He allowed the lack of provision to test our faith and ultimately grow it.

Complex Faith

Life is not simple. Faith is not simple. Far too often, we try to simplify it. We try to put God in a box, and we decide the rules. This is what God will do. This is what God won't do. That's never going to work. Our finite minds can never possibly hope to understand an infinite God.

On the other side of this, I look around and see God's goodness all around me. I trust Him more today than I did 18 months ago, but I don't see things the way I used to. If you go through a season of testing, don't expect me to toss out, "It will all be okay. God will provide." I don't throw those words around anymore. I know what it's like to have those words thrown at you when the person has absolutely no idea of what you are going through.

Instead, I will be the one to wrap my arms around

you and give you a hug. I won't have any words to say, because there aren't any. I will simply hurt with you and be with you in the moment. Then when I go home, I will write your name down in my journal and pray for you every morning until God gets you through your time of difficulty. And He will. I don't know when. I don't know how long it will be, but I know this season of testing will come to an end. You will see light again. Your heart will fill with joy once more. You will be able to laugh again. I know the One who is allowing you to go through this. He will take you to the very brink. He will risk you almost losing your faith so you can develop a deeper faith and relationship with Him. I know this because that's what He did with me.

Chapter Twenty-One

My Story is Still Being Written

We all want a miracle. We all want to write the book about God coming through miraculously for us. Nobody wants to be the one to write the book that says, "I'm still in my storm. God didn't answer my prayer the way I thought He would." Nobody wants their story to be, "We didn't get a miracle – we didn't get a baby, God didn't heal my loved one, my marriage couldn't be saved, we didn't buy our dream home, the pain hasn't stopped, we lost a family member to cancer, we had to shut the church down, we lost our foster baby, etc. God didn't answer our prayer." Nobody wants that to be his or her story, but that's sometimes how God works.

Mark Batterson

I want to tell you about two different people. The first person is a pastor by the name of Mark Batterson. He is an extremely successful pastor in the Washington, D.C. area who has accomplished amazing things for God. You may recognize his name from his books. He has several national bestsellers, but the one he is probably most famous for is his book, *The Circle Maker*. This book had such an incredible impact on me. If you haven't read it, I encourage you to read it and do the correlating Bible study. The book and the DVD study will forever change the way you pray. Mark Batterson has seen God do modern-day miracles in his church and in his own life. He teaches that we are not praying hard enough and circling things in prayer, and that's why we don't get blessings and answers from God in return.

Kara Tippetts

Next, I want to tell you about another person. Her name is Kara Tippetts. I never had the privilege of meeting her, but she forever changed my life. One date night, Matt and I ended up at a Barnes and Noble. We love going to Barnes and Noble, looking at books, getting a coffee from Starbucks, and sitting and reading for a little while. On this particular night, I was out of book suggestions and was combing the shelves of the Christian living section trying to find something to read. I picked up a book by Kara Tippetts called, *The Hardest Peace: Expecting Grace in the Midst of Life's Hard*. I stood in the Christian living section and didn't move for the next forty-five minutes. By the time Matt came and found me, I had tears streaming down my face and couldn't even talk to explain why I was crying.

The Hardest Peace tells the story of Kara Tippetts, a church planter's wife and mom of four young kids, who was diagnosed with cancer. She tells of days in bed wracked with pain, trying to spend as many moments as she could with her precious children while she was still able to. She writes about holding her kids while they cried and begged her not to leave them. I can't begin to tell you what that book did to me. A lot of books impact you, but every once in a while, you read a book that forever changes you. This book did

the Hidden Pain

just that for me. It touched me so deeply that it hurt to read it. It hurt to experience her life through her book. If you haven't read it, you need to. Let me warn you though, you will need an entire box of tissues. The heartbreaking end of the story is that Kara went home to heaven in 2015.

Mark Batterson and Kara Tippetts were contemporaries. One had his prayers answered and lives to inspire others to pray like it all depends on God and work like it all depends on you. He motivates and encourages thousands of people to pray more and watch God answer prayers. The other person, Kara, didn't get a miracle ending. Well ... actually, she did. She got to go to Heaven and be forever healed, but that's not what she was praying for. That's not what her husband and precious children prayed for. God's story for Kara's life was so different from Mark's story, yet she impacted just as many people. I believe we need both Mark Batterson's story and Kara Tippetts' story in our lives, because God works in both ways. He answers prayers, does miracles, and uses Mark Batterson to inspire a generation to still believe in and pray for miracles. But God also uses Kara Tippetts' story to remind us that even in the midst of life's hardest moments, He still loves us and has a plan for our lives. Kara's story impacts a generation to still believe in God's goodness, even when you can't see it. Her story inspires us to trust God no matter what.

Everybody wants to have a story of answered prayer and God's favor, but that doesn't always happen. Kara Tippetts' prayer for more time with her kids wasn't answered. Her kids' prayers that she would be healed didn't get answered in the way they wanted. Where is God in that? Nobody wants to write the story in which God doesn't come through and answer the prayer, but sometimes, that is exactly how life works.

Nobody wants to write a blog about staying faithful even when life is not going as we planned, but that's what God wants me to do. Nobody wants to pastor a church that isn't growing, but that's what we're doing.

We want answers; we want success. Is it just because we are not praying hard enough? Some Christian authors and preachers would say that things are not going forward simply because of that. Some pastors would say our church isn't taking off because we are not praying hard enough and fasting often enough.

the Hidden Pain

Others would say it's because we haven't worked hard enough. Still others would say we haven't trusted God enough – we don't have enough faith.

While we can grow in all of those areas and we can all pray more and have more faith, I don't think that's always the answer. I believe God works differently for different people. If we are not careful, these seemingly good ideas become very humanistic. Not praying hard enough, not fasting often enough, not working hard enough, not trusting God enough ... who does all of that rely on? Me. All of those things are dependent on me, not God.

I have dear friends who have begged God for a baby and haven't been able to have one, while other friends of ours praying for the same thing received their miracle baby. I have stood by the side of a dear friend who lost her grandson to cancer and held her as she wept. Matt has conducted the funeral for a young couple who lost their four-month-old baby. I begged God to heal my dear friend whose cancer came back a second time. Now I pray for her husband and two precious little boys who are left behind without their wife and mommy.

Where is God in the midst of absolute heartbreak? We can't even begin to understand. All we can do is choose to keep trusting. I believe God is sovereign both in what He does and in what He doesn't do, and He does both for a reason.

We have to choose to keep showing up, keep doing whatever it is God has called us to do. The story isn't over. God hasn't finished my story, and He hasn't finished yours. He won't be able to finish the work He started in and through us if we give up before the last page is written.

Chapter Twenty-Two

Rediscovering My Faith

I look back on some of the really dark moments of these past several years and feel like I've come out on the other side. I felt as if I'd lost my faith, but I discovered that it's been there all along. It's a small whisper of a beat, a thread. It's almost inaudible, almost severed, but it's still there. It still exists because God still exists, and He never left me. He's been there all along. Yes, He allowed me to go through a difficult season to figure out if I really trust Him and see if my faith is really strong enough. I had to be brought to the end of myself to find what's been there all along – God and the people around me. So, I stand up, push away the hurt, and look around me. Let me tell you what I see when I do that …

Let me tell you what our ministry looks like. We minister in the city. It's a dark place. We live by a no-name food store. It's not glamorous. It's dirty, old, worn-out, and beat-up – kind of like the people all around us. Life is hard. We deal with single moms who are left to care for their kids on their own. Sure, the ex is supposed to pay child support, but it's a broken system. They don't, and they get away with it. Then there's the wives of abuse who are broken, threatened, and seeking safety. There's those who have been sexually abused over and over again by those they trusted most, and now they can't trust anyone. They certainly can't trust a God who let this happen to them. There are the singles who just want to find someone to love them, the married couples who look good at church but things are going up in flames at home, those who are hopelessly addicted and can't fight anymore, the dear lady fighting cancer, the mom who lost her thirteen-year-old son, the grandma who lost her nineteen-year-old to cancer, the mom who lost her baby, the girl whose parents left her with a cult, the kid who is now grown up whose parents left him to survive alone with his siblings while they chased a life of drugs, and on and on the stories go.

All of these broken people show up at church. At *our* church, and we are supposed to help them. Me. The broken one who has struggled standing in her own faith. How in the world are we supposed to help them? I can't. Their pain and grief are more than I can handle. I don't have the answers. I sit and listen to their stories. I cry with them when I want to weep inside. I don't have any answers or comfort to give them.

Yet somewhere in the midst of this pain and suffering, I become the strong one. Me. The broken one, the weak one, the one who almost walked away from everything. I hug them, and with a touch, I try to let them feel Jesus through me. He is the only one who can get through to them, the only one who can give them peace, healing, and hope. In those moments, my pain is nothing compared to theirs, and I thank God for my blessings.

Our church is made up of completely broken people, and it's led by a broken pastor and his broken wife. Yet our brokenness leads to a different kind of church. Our church is a hospital, a place of healing. It's not out of the ordinary to see someone sitting and crying in our chairs before, during, or after the service. It's normal for Matt to talk about struggles in our personal lives. We don't put on a show. We don't come to church dressed to the nines in suits, heels, and nice dresses. We show up in jeans, t-shirts, and flip-flops. We are real because life is hard. We can't put on a show. This is real life, real pain, and it doesn't all go away just because we show up at church on Sunday morning.

Each Sunday, Matt reminds us from God's Word that we aren't without hope. Those who are strong that day encourage those who are weak. We talk about what we're going through and how we can go forward. We're reminded that it's not about us. It never was. It's about Jesus working in and through us. It's about holding on to faith for one more day, one more week, until God breaks through.

Every Sunday when I walk through the door of our church, I am reminded why we haven't walked away. These precious people are the reason we can't give up.

You see, these people are no longer just people to us. They have become our closest friends, our family – the people we do life with.

Our Growth Group

Every Tuesday night, eighteen people gather in our small home. It's our growth group. Every week, we sit around the tables with the adults at one table and the kids at another. With plates piled high with nachos, fajitas, meatball sandwiches, or whatever is on the menu for the week, we laugh together and talk about how our week is going. We spend time together praying and doing a Bible study. In our group, we've lost a baby and said goodbye to a mom, a dad, and a grandpa. We've been through hospital visits, pain, loss, and heartbreak. We've also celebrated the birth of two babies, rejoiced with pay raises and new jobs, and enjoyed countless birthday parties. Simply put, we do life together – the ups and downs, the good and the bad. We have become a family of sorts.

I am reminded of why we are doing what we are doing. It's simple. It's people – people who have become near and dear to our hearts. Each person that walks through the doors of our church walks out those same doors, carrying a piece of our heart with them. Matt and I don't do things half-hearted. We go all the way. So when God brings people our way, we give them all we have. Maybe we give too much of ourselves, and that's why we are so broken when people move on. We can't change that. That's just how God created us. So, we choose to love on whoever comes through the doors of Greater Philly Church for however long they choose to come, whether that's one Sunday or several years.

My Life Now

My life doesn't look anything like I thought it would when we began this adventure eight years ago. I thought things would look so different. I could never have anticipated the journey God would take us on. I would never have thought that this Christian-school girl with a Bible-college degree and a whole lot of faith would have been nearly broken. I am not the same person I was eight years ago, and I think that's a good thing.

Our life is far from ideal. It's not perfect. It's messy

and frustrating at times, but it's ours. It's the life God has given us to live, and I can either learn to embrace it or continue to be miserable. I've spent too much time being frustrated, overwhelmed, and brokenhearted. It's time to step away from that and live the life God has given me.

I can get so fixated on the problems of this life that I miss my blessings. Matt said recently, "If you focus so much on what you don't have, you lose sight of what you do have." I don't want that to be me!

It's been a long time, but I feel as if I'm finally healing. I can open my eyes and see God's goodness all around me. I see the sunrise each and every morning, reminding me that His compassions are new again today – His mercies are never ending. I look around at all the amazing people I get to live with and do life with, and I'm reminded that He didn't leave me alone. He gave me my amazing husband and precious children to laugh, play, work, and live life with. He gave me extended family and friends – the ones who call Greater Philly Church their own.

I also know that because of what we have gone through the last several years, God has given us opportunities that we wouldn't have had if things had gone differently. I know I wouldn't be blogging at Faithfully Stepping and trying to encourage other women in their journey of faith.

One of the things that I never saw coming was writing fiction. When I was young, I always thought it would be neat to be an author. I've always been a voracious reader, even when I was young. I told you about getting hooked on really good non-fiction books a few years into our church planting. Well, a few years ago, I decided to read the Harry Potter series to see what the fuss was all about. That sent me on a new journey of discovering the world of fantasy books.

Over the last few years, reading has allowed me to escape the days that felt too difficult to process my emotions. I really believe books helped keep me from making stupid decisions by just taking my mind off of the discouragement of my heart. I want to do that for somebody else.

So, I decided to give writing a try. I began writing my first fantasy fiction book, *Red Rose Rising*. I spent hours, days, and months working on that first fiction book and discovered something ... I love writing fiction!

If the church had taken off, I would never have discovered writing and encouraging people through my blog and books. I'm excited to see where it goes. It's not the plan I would have chosen, but God always has a better plan. Only God could take some dark moments in my life and use them to push me toward something that would breathe life into my soul.

Sometimes God Doesn't Take Our Problem Away

When our plans fall apart, our dreams die, and life hits us out of nowhere and knocks our feet out from under us, the first thing we do is call out to God to take it away. It's just too much. We can't handle the pressure, the heartbreak, the feelings of betrayal, the hurt, the stress, and on and on it goes. I've gone through this, and I have seen countless numbers of people go through this. We just want God to take it away. But more often than not, God doesn't. He doesn't remove the pain or the problem. Instead, He offers his grace to get through it.

The apostle Paul had a problem – a "thorn in the

the Hidden Pain

flesh" as he called it. He asked God to take it away several times, but God didn't. God's response to Paul is in II Corinthians 12:9, "And he said unto me, My grace is sufficient for thee: for my strength is made perfect in weakness. Most gladly therefore will I rather glory in my infirmities, that the power of Christ may rest upon me."

God doesn't promise to take our problems away. He says that His grace will be enough and His strength will be made perfect through our weakness. Somehow that's enough. It doesn't feel like it's enough when we are in the moment, but if we can stay faithful and trust God, He will get us through. Someday – maybe not today, maybe not a month from now or even a year from now, but someday, you will look back and see that God knew what He was doing all along. He was forming a new you, a better you.

So when you feel the hidden pain and you fear that God is no longer blessing your life … when you feel that your prayers are going unanswered, when you feel that God doesn't love you, when you beg for His help and He doesn't give it, and when He feels so far away, remember these words from someone who has gone through the same thing. God hasn't forgotten you. God loves you more than you can possibly know. He sees your hurt. He knows your fear and feels your pain. You will get through this. You will come out on the other side. Your faith will grow strong again. God is creating a new you, a stronger you. The new you is going to be unstoppable. Why do you think Satan is working so hard against you? Satan's greatest fear is a person in whom God has done His deepest work. That is going to be you on the other side of your hidden pain.

Conclusion

It's Time to Soar

I hope my story has been an encouragement to you. God has been working overtime on me. I feel like He just keeps hammering away at me. I don't know why other than He wants me to share with others what He has taught me. Doing so terrifies me, but I was reading a book a few months back that convinced me I needed to do just that. I was reading *Soar!* by T. D. Jakes. It is a fabulous book! One sentence especially caught my attention, "If you allow yourself to remain perched on the edge of life's nest, afraid to test your wings, then you risk missing out on becoming the person God made you to be."[22] I stopped after reading that sentence and knew I had to write this book. It scares me, but I don't want to sit around the rest of my life, too scared to step out and risk something for God. I do not want to miss out on becoming who God wants me to be.

So, it's my time to leave the comforts of the nest and fly. It's time to soar. The only reason I came to this place to be able to soar now is because I have dealt with my hidden pain. Just like Jacob of old, I have wrestled with God for His blessing. I feel like I have been wrestling with God these past several years, and I am choosing to use my pain as a ministry for others.

I don't know where you are. I don't know if you have been wrestling with God for a long time or if you are just starting your wrestling match. I can tell you that it's painful and hard; it will be more difficult than anything you have ever faced before. I can also tell you that if you can get through it, if you can hang in there until the night passes and the daylight begins, you will find yourself forever changed.

You won't be the same person who started the wrestling match with God. Let me warn you that you won't walk away unscathed. You will forever walk with a limp, but you will be proud of that limp because it signifies you were a God-wrestler. You wrestled with God and prevailed. Everyone that comes into contact with you will see your limp. They will see it's been hard – you've had grief, pain, physical problems, mental problems, and more hardship than anybody should have to bear. But they will also see the light in your eyes that only comes from wrestling with God Himself and receiving His blessing.

I don't know what hidden pain you are dealing with. I don't the hurt that is so deep and so private that you can't share it with anyone, but I know the hidden pain I have had. I know what it's like to feel as though God's favor has been removed from your life. I know what it's like to lay awake in fear in your bed at night. I know what it's like to plead with God to break through on your behalf. I know loneliness, I know shame, and I know the harsh judgment of others.

Yet I also know the beauty of a sunrise. A simple sunrise. A simple reminder that God is on His throne, and He got me through another long, dark night. Just as He got me through the long night, He will get me through this dark season of my life. He will carry me through, and I will look back on this season of life and know that I only got through it because He was carrying me.

I know the same to be true for you. God hasn't forgotten you. He is not ignoring you. He is not punishing you. God is working in you something far greater than making you feel "happy" right now. He is changing you into who He knows you can be. He doesn't want you to be the same person you were when your pain started. I don't have the answers for you. I don't know how long this is going to last. I don't know what you're going to lose or how you're going to be hurt. I only know the God Who is going to walk alongside you during it, and I trust Him to get you through.

He may go silent for a time, and you will be tempted to think He is no longer there – that He no longer cares. Don't let yourself believe that lie. It's not the truth, and it only hurts us in the long run. Deep down, we know God is still there. We just can't wrap our minds around why He is allowing certain things to happen in our lives.

The Sea of Galilee and the Dead Sea

I want to leave you with a parting illustration. I want to tell you about two bodies of water that are talked about a lot in the Bible. The first is the Sea of Galilee. The Jordan River flows into the Sea of Galilee, constantly dumping fresh water into it. The water flows through the Sea of Galilee and then flows out of it. This flow of water coming in and flowing out keeps it fresh. The land surrounding the Sea of Galilee is lush and verdant. Even mere pictures of it are stunning to look at.

The second body of water I want to call your attention to is the Dead Sea. Located only a little over 85 miles from the Sea of Galilee, the Dead Sea is appropriately named because nothing in or around it is alive. The Dead Sea is one of the saltiest bodies of water in the world. Why? Water flows into the Dead Sea but doesn't flow out. There is no outlet – nowhere for the water to go, so it sits and stagnates and begins to evaporate. Nothing can live in the Dead Sea. Actually, if you swim in the Dead Sea, you will float. Nothing sinks. If you look at pictures of the land surrounding the Dead Sea, it is a stark contrast to the land surrounding the Sea of Galilee. There is no vegetation, nothing living, and nothing green. Everything is dead.

The difference in the land surrounding these two bodies of water is astounding. Around the Sea of Galilee are lush, fertile fields. Around the Dead Sea is nothing but rocks. Why is that? The reason is the Sea of Galilee has water flowing in and out of it. The Dead Sea, however, has water flowing into it, but no water flowing out.

What is the point of all this? We all have hidden pain in our lives. We can choose to allow that pain to create hearts that are fertile and receptive to God, or we can have hearts that stagnate and die. To be like the Sea of Galilee, we need to pour our lives into other people. Love others, serve them, and take care of them. If we want to be like the Dead Sea, we just let other people serve us, love us, and take care of us; we just soak it all in but don't pour anything out on anybody else. A life spent living for myself is a wasted life. It's a waste of time and resources; it's a waste of love. I don't know about you, but I don't want the hidden pain in my life to go to waste, making me miserable and shriveled up. I want it to make me stronger.

I want it to mold me into who Jesus wants me to be. I want to be able to come alongside someone else and help them bear their pain so they no longer have to hide it.

Dealing With the Hidden Pain

We will know we have dealt with our hidden pain when we no longer question whether or not God is blessing our life. We will be able to look around at our life and see God's hand of blessing all around us. It may not be today, it may not be tomorrow. Take as long as you need to work through the process.

I don't know what the future holds for me, and I don't know what's in your future. But I know that God is working it for our good, and that's enough for today.

Bonus Chapter

How to Encourage Someone Going through a Difficult Season

One of the hardest things to know is how to help someone going through a hard time. There is nothing worse than somebody thinking they are helping you during a difficult season of life, and they are actually making it worse. I have heard so many horror stories of things people have said to someone when they are going through a hard time. My rule of thumb these days is to just keep quiet. When someone is going through a really difficult time, there is not much you can say that will help, and you will often just make things worse. Stick to things like, "I love you," "I'm praying for you," etc. For tangible ways to help, here are a few ideas:

1. Make a meal. When someone has been in the hospital, had a baby, lost a loved one, etc., a meal is always appreciated. A hot meal that you don't have to make yourself is a blessing to anyone.

2. Give money. There are very few people in the world who can't use an extra $50, especially if they are struggling financially. Even if you can't give a lot, don't ever underestimate the help your money can be. I can't tell you how many times a $50 bill or a $20 bill gave us money for groceries for the week. $50 can go a long way at an Aldi Grocery Store.

3. Send flowers. Sending flowers to someone just to let them know you are thinking of them and praying for them can really help. They can brighten anyone's day and are a reminder that they are not alone.

4. Send a card with your thoughts and prayers. Just reminding someone going through a hard time that you haven't forgotten them is an encouragement.

5. Buy groceries. You can even buy them online and have them sent right to their door. Having received groceries from other people several times, I can attest to what a blessing that can be.

Anything you choose to do for someone going through a hard time will be a blessing, no matter how big or small it is. We have had people send us checks in the mail, send us cash through an app, pay our mortgage, and/or a bill for us. People have brought groceries for us, taken us out to dinner, and on and on the list goes. Pray and ask God to show you how you can be a blessing to somebody going through a hard time. If you can't decide what to do, just ask them how you can help.

Acknowledgments

Thank you to Rebekah for many hours spent editing this book.

Thank you to my precious kiddos for being patient all the times mommy was busy writing. I love you!

Thank you to my husband, Matt for all the hours spent formatting this book and creating the amazing cover! Thank you also for being willing to walk alongside me on this journey. I wouldn't want to do this anybody else. Thank you for not giving up on me, our kids, or our church.

Endnotes

1. TerKeurst, Lisa. *Uninvited: Living Loved When You Feel Less Than, Left Out and Lonely.* (Nashville: Thomas Nelson, 2016), page 17.

2. Niequist, Shauna. *Present Over Perfect: Leaving Behind Frantic for a Simpler, More Soulful Way of Living.* (Grand Rapids, Michigan: Zondervan, 2016), 221.

3. Connelly, Jess and Hayley Morgan. *Wild and Free: A Hope-Filled Anthem for the Woman Who Feels She is Both Too Much and Never Enough.* (Grand Rapids, Michigan: Zondervan, 2016), 218.

4. Mateer, Julia. *Life-Giving Leadership: A Woman's Toolbox for Leading.* (Abilene, Texas: Leafwood Publishers, 2016), 44.

5. ibid., 194.

6. TerKuerst, Lisa. *Univited: Living Loved When You Feel Less Than, Left Out and Lonely.* (Nashville: Thomas Nelson, 2016), 114.

7. ibid., 143.

8. Lewis, C. S. The Four Loves. (New York, New York: Harper Collins Publishers, 1960).

9. Batterson, Mark. *The Circle Maker: Praying Circles Around Your Biggest Dreams.* (Grand Rapids, Michigan: Zondervan, 2011), 89.

10. Christianity Today Staff, "Fanny Crosby," Christianity Today, accessed November 20, 2019, https://www.christianitytoday.com/history/people/poets/fanny-crosby.html.

11. Worthington, Alli. Breaking Busy: How to Find Peace and Purpose in a World of Crazy (Grand Rapids, Michigan: Zondervan, 2016), page 103.

12. Ibid, 110.

13. Ibid., 103.

14. Batterson, Mark. *The Circle Maker: Praying Circles Around Your Biggest Dreams.* (Grand Rapids, Michigan: Zondervan, 2011), 89.

15. Mateer, Julia. *Life-Giving Leadership: A Woman's Toolbox for Leading.* (Abilene, Texas: Leafwood Publishers, 2016), 54,55.

16. Shankle, Melanie. *Church of Small Things: The Million Little Pieces that Make Up Life.* ((Grand Rapids, Michigan: Zondervan, 2017), 147.

17. Desert News Staff, "Top 100 C.S. Lewis Quotes," Deseret News Faith, June 27, 2012, https://www.deseretnews.com/top/817/61/Walking-Top-100-CS-Lewis-quotes-.html.

18. Ibid.

19. Allen, Jenni. Nothing to Prove: *Why We Can Stop Trying So Hard.* (Colorado Springs: Waterbrook Books, 2017), 224.

20. The Hollywood Film Critic. (2011, September 25) The Wisdom of C. S. Lewis (Blog Post) Retrieved from http://cslewiswisdom.blogspot.com/2011/09/it-is-not-your-business-to-succeed.html.

21. Burke, John. Imagine Heaven: Near-Death Experiences, God's Promises, and the Exhilarating Future that Awaits You (Grand Rapids, MI: Baker Books, 2015).

22. Jakes, T. D. *Soar! Build Your Vision from the Ground Up* (Dallas: TDJ Enterprises, 2017),

23. Allen, Jenni. *Nothing to Prove: Why We Can Stop Trying So Hard* (New York: Waterbrook, 2017), 224.

About the Author

Amanda Manney lives outside of Philadelphia with her husband and four kids. She and her husband started Greater Philly Church in 2011. Some of her favorite things to do include reading, family days, being a pastor's wife, and watching football on Sunday afternoons with her family.

Connecting with Amanda:
If you enjoyed this book, would you consider leaving me a review on Amazon? I would greatly appreciate it!

I would love to connect with you. You can find me on Facebook and Instagram at Faithfully Stepping. I would love to have you stop by my blog where you will find weekly inspirational posts. You can also receive a free copy of my ebook, *Better Mornings, Better Moms* by subscribing to my blog. You can find all this at Faithfullystepping.com.

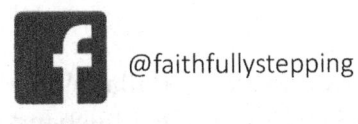

@faithfullystepping

@faithfullystepping_amanda

Be sure to grab my (free) eBook
Better Mornings, Better Moms at
www.FaithfullyStepping.com

Other Resources by Amanda Manney
Avaiable on Amazon

Faithfully Stepping Journal:

This six month journal uses an easy format to help you grow in your relationship with God using journaling, bible reading, and prayer time. The Faithfully Stepping Journal has three parts. The first section is for prayer and includes gratitude, confession, and requests for the day. The next section is for Bible reading. Here you record what you read for the day and journal about what impacted you. The last section is for writing down tasks or reminders for the day. Journaling daily will help to develop a consistency in your prayer life and Bible reading that will propel your spiritual growth to new levels.

Red Rose Rising:
(Fantasy/YA/Romance)

In an instant, she lost everything. He pulled her from the chaos, but she wants nothing to do with him.

Zalia's world was destroyed in an instant, her family and kingdom ripped away from her. She survives only because of the mysterious dark prince who saves her. Now she is on the run to save herself and to train to take back what was taken from her. She never expected he would be the one to help train her.

When Zalia turns eighteen, her powers manifest along with strange markings that are identical to the dark prince. It will take courage and opening her heart to love to fulfill the quest she has started.

Pillow Fights: Handling Marital Conflict Biblically (Christian Living/Relationships)

Marriage Conflict is not a question of if but when. Apart from God, a conflict has the power to destroy a marriage. *Pillow Fights* addresses conflicts that lead to the potential break-up of a marriage and the solutions to handling conflict according to God's Word.

    communicating with your spouse
    unmet expectations
    conflict in the bedroom
    how to fight fair
    conflict in front of your kids
    finding common ground
    and God's role in your marriage

You can have help and renewed hope for your marriage. Do not wait until it is too late to fix your marriage; learn to handle marital conflict today.